"As the world gets more connected, Sanjiv Chopra and Gina Vild remind us of the most important connection: with yourself."
—Bharat Anand, Henry R. Byers Professor of Business Administration, Harvard Business School, author *The Content Trap*

"Dr. Sanjiv Chopra and Gina Vild have created a pithy compilation of life meaning and purpose—a book you can open to any page on any day and find ways to manifest your unique path."
—Kyra Bobinet, M.D. MPH, author of *Well Designed Life*, CEO of engagedIN, consulting faculty, Stanford School of Medicine

"Vild and Chopra show exactly how to create happiness that is authentic, inspiring, and sustainable for anyone willing to open themselves to ask the questions and take the journey."
—Mark Bonchek, Ph.D., CEO of Shift Thinking

"Chopra and Vild prescribe a simple recipe of practicing Gratitude, Forgiveness, and Compassion to achieve Happiness. It is hard not to internalize it and accept it by the time you reach the end of the book."
—Desh Deshpande, serial entrepreneur, founder of Deshpande Center for Technological Innovation at MIT

"The most practical, comprehensive, and evidence-based guide to happiness I've ever read! A must-read that can change your life!"
—Elan Divon, author, spiritual teacher, and cofounder of The Einstein Legacy Project and Genius 100 Visions, the world's first 3D printed book

"This fun book offers practical advice to help you become a happier and more fulfilled person. In the process you may actually end up making the world a better place for all."
—Peng Fan, M.D., professor of Clinical Medicine, David Geffen School of Medicine at UCLA

"A true gift you will both richly enjoy and want to share with others."
—Lachlan Forrow, M.D., Beth Israel Deaconess Medical Center, Harvard Medical School, President Emeritus, The Albert Schweitzer Fellowship

"A must-read for anyone committed to their own happiness and the happiness of those they love."
—Adrian Wilkins, author of *The Way of the Superior Dentist*

THE
TWO MOST
IMPORTANT DAYS

Also by Sanjiv Chopra

*The Big Five: Five Simple Things You Can Do
to Live a Longer, Healthier Life*

Dr. Sanjiv Chopra's Liver Book (with Sharon Cloud Hogan)

*Dr. Chopra Says: Medical Facts and Myths Everyone Should
Know* (with Dr. Alan Lotvin)

*Leadership by Example: The Ten Key Principles of All Great
Leaders* (with David Fisher)

Brotherhood: Dharma, Destiny, and the American Dream
(with Deepak Chopra)

THE
TWO MOST
IMPORTANT DAYS

HOW TO FIND YOUR PURPOSE—
AND LIVE A HAPPIER,
HEALTHIER LIFE

SANJIV CHOPRA

and

GINA VILD

Thomas Dunne Books
St. Martin's Press
New York

THOMAS DUNNE BOOKS.
An imprint of St. Martin's Press.

THE TWO MOST IMPORTANT DAYS. Copyright © 2017 by
Sanjiv Chopra and Gina Vild. All rights reserved. Printed
in the United States of America. For information, address
St. Martin's Press, 175 Fifth Avenue, New York, N.Y. 10010.

www.thomasdunnebooks.com
www.stmartins.com

The Library of Congress Cataloging-in-Publication Data is
available upon request.

ISBN 978-1-250-11936-0 (hardcover)
ISBN 978-1-250-11937-7 (ebook)

Our books may be purchased in bulk for promotional,
educational, or business use. Please contact your local
bookseller or the Macmillan Corporate and Premium Sales
Department at 1-800-221-7945, extension 5442, or by email
at MacmillanSpecialMarkets@macmillan.com.

First Edition: December 2017

10 9 8 7 6 5 4 3 2 1

"The two most important days in your life are the day you are born and the day you find out why."

—MARK TWAIN

To Amita, a beautiful, brilliant, and spiritual person. You raised our children with pure love. You're a paragon of virtue and wisdom. I am grateful to you for bringing so much happiness to our shared journey and helping me define and live my purpose in life.

◆

To Gillian and Gareth, with so much gratitude for your huge good hearts. You enrich all who know you with your wisdom, wit and sparkle. Being your mother is my most joyful purpose.

CONTENTS

CONTENTS

ACKNOWLEDGMENTS

This book reflects the tapestry of our lives. It conveys the philosophies we live by, the poetry that inspires us, and the lessons we've learned along the way and wish to pay forward.

We are deeply grateful for those who have cheered us along this path, offering insights, goodwill, and nuggets of inspiration. Their encouragement enriches this book and our lives.

Thomas Dunne, our publisher at St. Martin's Press, for your believing in this book when it was merely a glimmer in our eye.

Amanda Annis, our literary agent at Trident Media Group, for your rich literary sensibility and for giving form to our endeavor.

Emily Angell and Lisa Bonvissuto, our editors at St. Martin's Press, for your sage editing and gentle hands that guided our many suggestions back to your point of view and made us realize you were right all along.

Stephanie Shorter, for your brilliant research and your enduring enthusiasm.

Meta Wagner, for your valued friendship and for illuminating our path by sharing with us your own literary journey.

Louise Roslansky, for the gift of your friendship and for cheering us up and on with your luminous presence.

Brian Atchison, Adrian Wilkinson, Kathy Bickimer, John McNeil, Venkat Srinivasan, and Paul Rufo, for serving as a focus group of one whenever called upon, for your sage advice and your treasured friendship.

Dorothy and John Vild, for guiding me even in your absence, and for the memory of your deep love and unshakable belief that I could do anything.

Gillian Rulewski and Gareth Rulewski, for being the wellspring of my happiness—my two most important days were the days you were born.

Nigel Rulewski, for encouraging me from the get go to write this book and for your absolute certainty that I could do it.

Krishan and Pushpa Chopra, for your core values and philosophies, which are threaded throughout this book and infused in my life and Deepak's.

Deepak Chopra, my loving brother, for being a force of inspiration.

Amita Chopra, for feeding us your wisdom, love, and culinary delights too numerous to count.

Priya, Bharat and Donna, Kanika and Sarat, and my grandchildren Aanya and Mira, for being such luminous jewels in my life and inspiring me in countless ways.

Our treasured family and friends—you know who you are—our gratitude is deep and wide. Our shared journey is a magnificent gift.

"Our True Heritage"
Thích Nhất Hạnh

The cosmos is filled with precious gems.
I want to offer a handful of them to you this morning.
Each moment you are alive is a gem,
shining through and containing earth and sky,
water and clouds.

It needs you to breathe gently
for the miracles to be displayed.
Suddenly you hear the birds singing,
the pines chanting,
see the flowers blooming,
the blue sky,
the white clouds,
the smile and the marvelous look
of your beloved.

You, the richest person on Earth,
who have been going around begging for a living,
stop being the destitute child.
Come back and claim your heritage.
We should enjoy our happiness
and offer it to everyone.
Cherish this very moment.
Let go of the stream of distress
and embrace life fully in your arms.

INTRODUCTION

"The two most important days in your life are the day you are born and the day you find out why," Mark Twain famously wrote.

Time is a currency, and *how* you spend it and *with whom* you spend it are the most important decisions you will ever make. Time is precious and short, yet there is time enough to do something meaningful. There is time enough to find your singular life purpose, one that will both enrich your existence and improve the lot of those who travel along on this shared journey.

We wrote this book out of recognition that life without purpose is a shallow pool, an aimless meandering through the days and months from birth to death. While it is true that every life will have bursts of happy moments, we should have greater aspirations. We know that a life inspired by an awareness of the vast possibilities is a life that is truly vibrant and one that enables sustained happiness.

Today, everywhere you look, there are books, articles, interviews, presentations, and conversations about happiness. Researchers bombard us with data that promise to point the way. Chatter about happiness is inescapable. It's everywhere. And as scientists, philosophers, and experts pontificate, we clamor to understand. We seek any wisdom that will show us how to find it. A search on Amazon turns up nearly two hundred thousand books related to happiness. Yes, we all seem to be on a quest to be happy.

Yet the path to happiness is really quite simple. Look no further. Here is your map. Right here is everything you need to know.

Happiness is a by-product of being present to witness your life and ultimately identifying your life's purpose. You will find happiness by listening—really listening—to music, by reflecting on the musings of poets, by paying attention to the scenes and sounds of nature, by accessing the stillness within yourself through meditation, and by surrounding yourself with kindred spirits—and if they like to laugh, it's a bonus. Happiness is a result of first looking inward and then gazing outward. It's about using your time to make the journey of others a little bit better. You can be of service merely by being present and paying attention to the needs of others. As the poet Julia Kasdorf wrote:

> I learned that whatever we say means nothing,
> what anyone will remember is that we came. . . .
> To every house you enter, you must offer
> Healing: a chocolate cake you baked yourself,
> the blessing of your voice, your chaste touch.[1]

This is all you need to know: *happiness is a choice.* By finding your life's purpose, you are choosing a happy life. This book will explore how you can live a life with purpose. Our promise to you is that you will be inspired, and best of all, you will have fun.

We will share with you the transformative power of gratitude, forgiveness, and serving others. We suggest films, TED Talks, books, apps, and songs to boost your HQ—your happiness quotient. We offer exercises to prod your thinking and poetry to ignite your sense of wonder.

The concept for this book was sparked when Sanjiv was asked to give an academic talk on dharma, happiness, and living with purpose. To prepare, he sought input from friends and family. He asked Gina, a colleague at Harvard Medical School, to contribute her thoughts. She mused over the topic and reached out to her friends, who offered personal wisdom and reflection, some of it to be found within these pages. A partnership of kindred spirits coalesced, and our research continued, culminating in this book. It has been a happy journey filled with purpose.

We hope that this book finds a home on your bedside table and becomes a lasting resource that you will return to again and again. If we have been successful, after reading this book, you will radiate happiness, making others happier too.

We hope to convince you that a happy life, a life lived with purpose, will not be found in bling, souped-up cars, and fancier clothes. In short, it cannot be found in "more."

Rather, happiness will be found in saying "thank you" and "I forgive you." It can be found in simply supporting a school car wash, volunteering at a homeless shelter, or campaigning for a candidate who shares your values. It can be found by spending time with friends, listening to music, and meditating. You will learn, if you don't already know this, that gratitude, forgiveness, and service to others are catalysts for resilience. With these behaviors at your core, you will sharpen your thinking and find your way to a radiant life of happiness, joy, and bliss. Pablo Picasso thought of it in this way: "The meaning of life is to find your gift. The purpose of life is to give it away."

In these pages, we offer expert scientific research and share the distilled experiential wisdom from friends and colleagues as well as our own personal reflections. By retelling the stories of those who have found their life's purpose after witnessing tragedy or after being inspired by the good work of others, we hope to lay down a foundation upon which you can build as you explore the wonders of life's many possibilities.

At the core of this foundation is an understanding that as you seek uplifting experiences—as you reach for happiness—life will at times push back and thwart your progress, hand you sorrow, and toss challenges in your path. On some days, you'll find the road feels endless and dark. We hope to show you that on these days it is best to accept adversity and reach within yourself for resilience.

As Albert Camus so eloquently said, "In the midst of winter, I found there was, within me, an invincible summer. And that makes me happy. For it says that no matter how hard the world pushes against me, within me, there's something stronger—something better, pushing right back."

So jump headfirst into this book. There's no need to read it front to back. Open to any chapter and inhale the poetry, ponder over the exercises, mull over the stories. Talk it over with family and friends. Use the wisdom found here to navigate your way to a life of purpose and happiness.

We believe that to find lasting sustained happiness, we each need to discover our own singular purpose in life and then pursue it with unbridled passion. That's part of the secret: the passion. We invite you to take the plunge, realize your passion, and be happy.

"Sonnets to Orpheus, Part Two, XII"
Rainer Maria Rilke

Want the change. Be inspired by the flame
where everything shines as it disappears.
The artist, when sketching, loves nothing so much
as the curve of the body as it turns away.

What locks itself in sameness has congealed.
Is it safer to be gray and numb?
What turns hard becomes rigid
and is easily shattered.

Pour yourself like a fountain.
Flow into the knowledge that what you are seeking finishes
*   often at*
the start, and, with ending, begins.

Every happiness is the child of a separation
it did not think it could survive. And Daphne, becoming
*   a laurel,*
dares you to become the wind.

—*In Praise of Mortality*, translated and edited by
Anita Barrows and Joanna Macy

1

What Does It Mean to Live with Purpose?

I felt once more how simple and frugal a thing is happiness: a glass of wine, a roast chestnut, a wretched little brazier, the sound of the sea. Nothing else.
—NIKOS KAZANTZAKIS

Happiness. Life's holy grail. It is both the ends and the means, the alpha and the omega, the blue highway to satisfaction and the destination sought by each of us rambling travelers. People go to unimaginable lengths to chase happiness—choose careers to make big money, spend that big money, look for love in others, poke around every nook and cranny of life—often to discover that happiness remains perennially elusive. Others forgo the quest to seek out happiness and do nothing more than walk the beach with friends, change diapers while humming to the baby, and volunteer at an animal shelter, only to find that happiness is their ever-present companion.

The search for happiness is hardwired into our DNA. The yearning is universal, transcending age, gender, geography, vocation, and personal circumstances. Throughout history, it has been a lifelong pursuit. It is a journey that is as rich as the destination is rewarding.

It was once believed that happiness was in the domain of a select few—the kings, nobles, poets, and philosophers. Socrates argued that this was not the case and that happiness could be achieved through human endeavor. He fiercely believed that virtue and happiness were inextricably linked. In fact, the ancient Greeks had a word for happiness. They referred to it as human flourishing, and they called it *eudaimonia*. The Sanskrit word for this, for happiness and bliss, is *Ananda*.

Too frequently, people look for happiness in all the wrong places. They turn to external factors. Everyone loves to be rewarded for a job well done, so it is easy to associate the reward of happiness with some sort of indulgence, such as drinking French champagne or driving a Tesla.

But it is important to remember, happiness is more than the sum total of happy moments.

When you feel that warm glow from opening a present, it makes you happy, right? But is it the item inside that makes you happy, or the fact that it was a gift from someone who cares? This is where the pursuit of happiness gets muddled. People think that a happier life is the result of having more money, acquiring things (expensive vacations, mansions, jewelry), being promoted at work, and receiving praise.

What many chasers of ephemeral pleasure do not realize is that central to having a happy life is living a life of purpose. This isn't just a sweet sentiment or the sum of a millennia of anecdotes and aphorisms. Philosophers across time have proposed this idea, with little evidence aside from strong logic and obvious examples of noble lives well lived. So, Søren Kierkegaard, you say we create ourselves by our choices? Prove it, we say. Where are the data?

To flourish is to truly thrive—not just to get along, not just to survive, not even just to be happy. It means to feel a connection with your life in a meaningful way that leads to physical, social, and spiritual rewards. Flourishing is to grow without boundaries, to be unstoppable in your power, to soar to your heights that resonate deep within you.

Today, people like to see hard evidence before accepting beneficent advice, and the world's scientific community has risen to the challenge by studying happiness and the range of one's emotional response. Contained within these pages are the conclusions of myriad scientists who have studied happiness and a variety of interesting factors that have been shown to contribute to it. The results of these scientific studies will boost your awareness and growth. Ultimately, however, lasting happiness is an inside job. Keep that in mind. It is up to you to find your unique purpose in life and live it with exuberant passion.

THE HUMAN CONDITION

There is more hunger for love and appreciation in this world than for bread.

—MOTHER TERESA

The saint of Calcutta, Mother Teresa, saw a wider range of happiness and despair than many of us can even imagine. Her personal path to bliss involved nothing but sacrifice and a single-minded devotion to everyone but herself. Mother Teresa spent her life in the most destitute slums in the world, yet the images that we find in the pages of *Time* and *National Geographic* show beatific smiles not only on her face but also on the faces of those poor and mostly forgotten children and adults who surrounded her wherever she went. By serving others throughout her life, Mother Teresa achieved the ultimate goal: attaining deep and lasting happiness.

Helping others to flourish lays the foundation for psychological growth. But what does it mean to flourish? Can you have happy moments and not flourish? Can you be professionally successful but not be happy? Let's take a moment to go over some basic terminology regarding the human condition as it pertains to happiness, joy, and bliss.

To flourish is to truly thrive—not just to get along, not just to survive, not even just to be happy. It means to feel a connection with your life in a meaningful way that leads to physical, social, and spiritual rewards. Flourishing is to grow without boundaries, to be unstoppable in your power, to soar to your heights that resonate deep within you. It means that every day you wake up is a day when you will become an even better you and that will transform the people and world around you. When you flourish, your inner light will be brighter, and you will radiate happiness.

Flourishing encompasses happiness, joy, and bliss, as well as the more immediate sensations of pleasure and satiation. Pleasure and satiation are often mistaken for what nurtures the human spirit. Pleasure refers to the senses more than the mind. Although we may find something pleasing and it may bring us good feelings, the term *pleasure* conjures images of events and things that give us a quick thrill. It is the positive side of an evolutionary driving force, the effort to seek what feels good and avoid what feels not so good. Satiation is simply eliminating negative feelings of desire. Is it possible to oversatiate oneself? Who hasn't had too much chocolate? It is important to recognize that trying to satiate your deepest desires with a quick fix is at the core of many troublesome addictions. A purposeful life leads to happiness, but satiation does not.

Happiness can mean a state of well-being or joy prompted by a variety of things, such as recognition, praise, a good round of golf, immersion in a page-turner of a novel, a day off from work, sitting on a porch swing. These things often can make you happy in the moment, and almost certainly you look forward to replicating these experiences. Happiness represents a range of good feelings, from mild contentment to rapturous joy. You can think of happiness as the warm glow accompanying well-being. Happiness can be a fire that smolders or one that bursts into ascending and dancing flames.

Joy is a temporary state of intense happiness. It is often linked to the deep pleasure you get when you achieve success after working hard toward a goal. It is an exuberant but brief feeling. Dancing at a concert may bring joy when exercise, music, and friendship all converge. The expression on a child's face when he blows out birthday candles and makes a wish is joyful. Getting that 4.0 and delivering your valedictorian speech will cause intense *joy*, while working steadily toward that goal made you *happy*.

Bliss is the key that unlocks the door to lasting happiness. Bliss is reflected in how we are intertwined with friends and family and experience reciprocal love and connection. Bliss is feeling love toward others and being grateful for the world around you. It is feeling known—and knowing another—at the deepest level. These kindred connections offer a glimpse into what it means to be human. Bliss is experiencing the birth of a child or grandchild and feeling your place in the march of time, seeing the promise of generations to come, providing you with a peek into your future lineage. Bliss is being at your place of worship, be it a church, temple, or coffeehouse, and feeling the ambient connection to the like-minded folks surrounding you, praying the same prayers, drinking the same mochas.

Here it is, succinctly stated. Happiness is the road you

walk on, joy is the beautiful landmarks you see along your way, and bliss is being grateful for the journey and conveying that gratitude to your grandchildren, lover, or those who share your path.

FEELING KNOWN

When we greet someone here in America, we usually just say "Hello" or "Good morning." It is a simple greeting and, for the most part, without deep meaning. The Zulu, however, have a more meaningful greeting. One person will greet the other with "Sikhona," which means, *I am here to be seen*.[1] It's a proclamation of your presence, your desire to be recognized. In reply, the other will say "Sawubana," meaning, *I see you*. This response is an open recognition of the other's being, but this person is also expressing his or her respect for the other. The greeting makes evident the willingness of the individuals to inhabit that single moment with all their being.

If only we could all be so open and acknowledge our vulnerability. We all need to be known, to be recognized by our peers, by our loved ones, by everyone, blemishes and all.

You may be familiar with the next example, a common greeting in India—*Namaste*.[2] The word is derived from *namah*, meaning *bow*; and *te*, meaning *to you*. *I bow to you*. It's usually spoken while bowing, palms together, fingers toward the heavens. *Namaste*, on a deeper level, means, *I bow to the divine in you*. It's a gesture of respect, of one soul recognizing another, a greeting eschewing thought of race and gender and focusing purely on the truth of *we are one*.

Happiness is the road you walk on, joy is the beautiful landmarks you see along your way, and bliss is being grateful for the journey and conveying that gratitude to your grandchildren, lover, or those who share your path.

Namaste is integral to a state in which people *feel recognized and known* and, while recognizing and understanding others, this state of being is integral to everyday happiness. Consider as an example a jovial man with a mail route in a largely rural area. "The people make my heart swell," he said. "I see them every day, but they never fail to recognize the happiness I bring, and I always appreciate the happiness they give me. Daily. And they don't even know it," he ended with a laugh. Without know it, he was conveying meaning of the Zulu words *sikhona* and *sawubana*, and he was only just short of greeting everyone, and his *hello* to those along his route was equivalent to *namaste*.

This path to happiness isn't always easy because we are often taught from a young age to be strong, to not show vulnerability. Showing vulnerability can go against our very grain. It takes great courage to be open to others, to open ourselves to the world. Yet if we can be comfortable allowing others to know us with all our individual complexities, we will be one step closer to happiness.

The poet Ted Hughes said, "The only calibration that counts is how much heart people invest, how much they ignore their fears of being hurt or caught out or humiliated. And the only thing people regret is that they didn't live boldly enough, that they didn't invest enough heart, didn't love enough. Nothing else really counts at all."

We couldn't have said it better ourselves.

Or maybe we can—*namaste*.

THE SCIENCE OF JOYFUL PURPOSE

The purpose of life is not to be happy. It is to be useful, to be honorable, to be compassionate, to have it make some difference that you have lived and lived well.

—RALPH WALDO EMERSON

If you try to chase happiness without having a clear idea of what happiness is, you are destined to fail because you tend to pursue things that are ephemeral and provide only short-term pleasure. When you approach happiness with an understanding that it is connected to purpose and to contributing in some way to the betterment of those around you, you will succeed.

9

Choosing wisely will lead you to the best path to happiness. You can use the power of decision-making to choose activities, friends, and mind-sets that will pave the way to a purposeful and happy life. Today and every day, you have total control of your life choices, and they affect every aspect of your tomorrows.

Here it is in four simple words: happiness is a choice.

Happiness advice may be dismissed as nothing more than platitudes and overworked proverbs, but, in fact, there is a robust body of science that helps us understand the physiological, neurochemical, and behavioral underpinnings of happiness. The good news is that science has stripped away much of the mystery surrounding what prompts us to feel contentment, happiness, and joy. Once we understand the science, we can reach for simple tools that have proven beneficial.

Here it is in four simple words: happiness is a choice.

The French existentialists had quite a lot to say about choice and living a purpose-driven life. In fact, they theorized that our lives are wholly defined by our choices and that who we are at our core is not set at birth, but rather determined by the choices we make. Author Rick Riordan has something to say about it too: "That's the nice thing about being human. We only have one life, but we can choose what kind of story it's going to be."

Think of it like this: We are born a pillar of exquisite marble. From this we carve our essential self. Our purpose is not given to us like a prize at a raffle. Our purpose is defined by our choices. Consider the following.

There is a scientific formula to calculate your happiness quotient (HQ). This formula was a revelation made by Sonja Lyubomirsky, Ken Sheldon, David Schkade, and Martin Seligman, who studied identical twins separated at birth. They created a formula that explains the three factors that determine your level of happiness—biology, living conditions, and voluntary actions.[3]

Their study indicated that 50 percent of your happiness quotient is inherited and considered a set point. Your set point is defined by the state where you balance, where you tend to fall despite the varied ups and downs of life.

Of the remaining 50 percent of your happiness quotient, 10 percent is dependent upon your living conditions and how satisfying they are.

An astounding 40 percent of your happiness quotient, as it turns out, is the result of voluntary actions—how you *choose* to live your life. Do you volunteer? Do you use your life to make the world a better place? Are you a supportive and compassionate friend? Do you tend to think only of yourself, or are you concerned about those with whom you share your life's journey? If you make choices that put others first, these choices will lead you to a life defined by purpose.

The surprising bonus of this behavior is that by reaching out, you in turn enrich your own life. Using your life as a gift to others will make *you* happy. It's a gift you give that gives back. This may seem counterintuitive, that helping others leads to your own happiness, but there is an abundance of evidence—we're just passing it on to help make this a kinder, happier world.

An interesting side note to all of this is that beyond being able to boost your HQ through voluntary actions of compassion and service, you can actually increase your HQ genetic set point. You can alter it by the simplest practice of all—by expressing gratitude.

In fact, Robert Emmons conducted a fascinating study. Individuals were assigned to one of three groups. One group wrote down each day for ten weeks five things they were grateful for. The second group wrote down each day for ten weeks five things that displeased them. The third group wrote down each day for ten weeks five neutral events. Those in the first group felt better about their lives as a whole and were more optimistic about the future than those in the other two groups. Astoundingly, the group that expressed daily gratitude increased their happiness level by 25 percent. This study further demonstrates that the genetic set point is malleable and dynamic.[4]

Gratitude? Is it true that saying *thank you* will make you happier?

That's right. Your mother gave you an important life skill when she made you write all those thank-you notes. Gratitude has been scientifically linked to better heart health, a feeling of contentment and calm, and lower cortisol levels. Really, all this by just saying, "Thank you."[5]

FAILURE AND ADVERSITY

As we find our way in life and make daily choices, it's necessary to learn to embrace failure. Yes, failure can be good. You can learn from it. It can serve as a transformative life force.

The commencement speech given by J. K. Rowling, author of the *Harry Potter* series, at Harvard in 2008 reflected on her personal story and her awareness of how failure made her life better, how failure was a catalyst for her remarkable success.

> So why do I talk about the benefits of failure? Simply because failure meant a stripping away of the inessential. I stopped pretending to myself that I was anything other than what I was, and began to direct all my energy into finishing the only work that mattered to me. Had I really succeeded at anything else, I might never have found the determination to succeed in the one arena I believed I truly belonged. I was set free, because my greatest fear had been realized, and I was still alive, and I still had a daughter whom I adored, and I had an old typewriter and a big idea. And so rock bottom became the solid foundation on which I rebuilt my life.[6]

She added,

> Failure gave me an inner security that I had never attained by passing examinations. Failure taught me things about myself that I could have learned no other way. I discovered that I had a strong will, and more discipline than I had suspected; I also found out that I

had friends whose value was truly above the price of rubies.

This stupendously successful author seized the opportunity of her failure to strip away all the distracting details of her life and focus on what was truly meaningful to her. Understanding who you at your core is virtually impossible to do without experiencing failure. A life of personal growth and outstanding success is only possible by experiencing failure.

What J. K. Rowling learned and shared with us is that adversity can be a gift. Adversity can lead you to one of life's greatest resources—resilience. But we don't have to hit rock bottom to learn from our failures. When we begin to accept setbacks and learn from them, whether small or large, only then do we embrace the gift of adversity and gain resilience.

Resilience is born from learning how to bounce back from disappointments. Perhaps a relationship didn't turn out as you had hoped. Maybe you were laid off from your job. Possibly you had a quarrel with a friend. Remember the earlier discussion of choice? Well, you have a choice to make when these situations present themselves. You can choose to spiral into self-pity, victimhood, or sadness, or you can choose to accept these events as opportunities and use them to alter your path. You can decide to use the knowledge garnered from the experience to learn and to grow. The loss and unhappiness will inevitably result in personal growth.

Martha N. Beck and her husband both had two Harvard degrees apiece when Martha became pregnant with their second child and learned their unborn son had Down syndrome.

Martha grappled with the difficult news and had the wisdom to turn her adversity into a gift. "*This is it*, I thought. *This is the part of us that makes our brief, improbable little lives worth living: the ability to reach through our own isolation and find strength, and comfort, and warmth for and in each other. This is what human beings do. This is what we live for, the way horses live to run.*" She later chronicled her experience and the insights she garnered in a bestselling memoir, *Expecting Adam*.

Not all difficulties are experienced on such a grand scale. Take, for example, a professional setback. What if you were fired from your job? That's a wallop of a disappointment. How do you handle it? You can choose to cry, and maybe you should for a day. But you can also choose to examine whether there might be lessons learned. Ask yourself, did you not work hard enough? Did you slack off? Were you the victim of a political battle between two colleagues? Is there anything you could have done to remediate the situation before you lost your job?

The answer to one or more of these questions may be yes. How could this new awareness impact your future? Could you build on the experience and make certain you avoid the same mistakes in your next job? Could you use the job loss to ask yourself if this is the best field for you? Might this be a eureka moment that sets you on a new professional path?

Sometimes the difficult experience, whatever it is, makes you realize you must soldier forth. As a writer, for instance, if you give up after your first rejection notice, you'll never find success. If you cough and splutter that first time in the pool, haul yourself out, and say, "I'm never going to swim again," then yes, you're probably right. You won't.

You have a choice, and the best choice is to make a conscious choice to bounce back.

A last word on adversity from J. K. Rowling:

> The knowledge that you have emerged wiser and stronger from setbacks means that you are, ever after, secure in your ability to survive. You will never truly know yourself, or the strength of your relationships, until both have been tested by adversity. Such knowledge is a true gift, for all that it is painfully won, and it has been worth more than any qualification I ever earned.[7]

Think about it. Failure is fundamental to our growth from the time we are infants. Parents confront this as they stand by watching their baby fall as it tries to take its first steps. The loving parents must accept that their baby will fall as a necessity before it can learn to walk. Without falling over, time and again, how would a baby learn balance? Staying upright is only possible after falling teaches a baby to find its tipping point. Failing hurts. It hurts our feelings, hurts our pride, and in some cases, hurts our bottoms.

We all tend to avoid painful stimuli, so it is natural that we go to great lengths to avoid falling or failing. However, this avoidance can lead us to insulate ourselves against not just failure but success as well. If we don't get in the game, we can't win the game. When we don't play, we don't win. The trite phrase "practice makes perfect" implicitly means, "Everyone loses until they don't."

Failure is opportunity knocking—really hard. As a prisoner of war and now motivational speaker, Captain Charlie Plumb said, "Adversity is a terrible thing . . . to waste." Think of it as a wake-up call or a character-building experience; failure serves as an excellent learning tool, perhaps the most powerful one known.

Norman E. Rosenthal calls adversity the "best teacher most of us will ever encounter."[8] Our lives are given greater meaning when we have adversity to challenge us and turbulence to propel us forward. Our failures are the notches on the door by which we measure our growth.

Not succeeding has led to the success of countless individuals and the human race in general—provided you survive, that is. Evolution is founded on failure, and the results are spectacular. Due to failure, sperm whales have evolved to dive deeper than most submarines, and birds have evolved their feathers to blend as camouflage with their native environment.

All failure doesn't have to be personal. Thanks to the ability to learn by watching others, we can sometimes benefit from failure without suffering it ourselves. However, the act of failing is still necessary. *Someone* must flop for the rest of us to succeed. Perhaps that is why we love heroes who have flaws. Many identify with hubris because we have all felt the terrible jaws of its consequences. We get to watch and learn. Those who fail are a cautionary tale for those of us who were thinking about taking a snow tube up the double-black-diamond ski run until we searched "snow tube fails" on YouTube.

As leadership consultant Bud Bilanich notes, "Failure is an outcome." There are several ways any endeavor can go, and sometimes things don't pan out the way you thought they would. However, don't immediately assume that an unexpected ome is a failure. Often there are multiple ways to win; it just takes some creative vision to make lemonade out of the lemons you were handed.

It's important to remember as you embrace failure that you shouldn't be too hard on yourself. Remember life is a journey and that failing teaches you exactly what *not* to do in the future. It helps you focus on alternative solutions. Bilanich recommends that the next time you fail, you ask yourself five questions:

As a prisoner of war and now motivational speaker, Captain Charlie Plumb said, "Adversity is a terrible thing . . . to waste."

---

1. Why did I fail? What did I do to cause the failure?
2. What could I have done to prevent the failure?
3. What have I learned from this situation?
4. What will I do differently the next time?[9]

Begin at once to live, and count each separate day as a separate life.

—SENECA

Thomas Edison had a good perspective when reflecting on the trials and tribulations of inventing the lightbulb. He said, "I have not failed. I've just found ten thousand ways that won't work."

Studying what went wrong has become something of a science in recent years. Management workshops and inspirational posters alike tout the virtues of belly-flopping. Entrepreneurship focuses on recognizing critical aspects of business and the make-and-break factors.

Entrepreneurs tend to be go-getters, and they have taken the study of failure to a professional level. At the annual Fail-Con gathering, entrepreneurs reflect on one another's mistakes with a fine-tooth comb, happily instructing themselves and others on how *not* to do business. This whole discipline is divided equally between the study of success and the study of failure, with both rolled up into the term *opportunity*. Opportunity recognition is crucial to new venture creation, and this involves seeing the need to innovate around providing a service while navigating potential pitfalls lurking around the bend.

Another way to look at failure is through the lens of a crisis, which, by definition, is a time when a difficult decision must urgently be made. The Chinese symbol for *crisis* is comprised of two characters: *danger* and *opportunity*. The ancient Chinese knew a thing or two about the mercurial nature of crises. They understood that a catastrophe can also be an opportunity; life can look vastly different when you change your perch.

In short, a crisis offers us opportunity for a good outcome. Our challenge is to find the path that leads us there.

We all fear failure, but perhaps this is *because it is good for us*. Failure is a growing experience, and growth is synonymous with growing pains. Can these growing pains ever be enjoyed? How about working out? Dieting? Cleaning the garage? Yet when we embrace this, we are invariably stronger and better prepared to face life and to thrive.

Most of us will experience sorrow in our lives, sometimes profound sorrow. When we emerge from that dark abyss of loss and pain with a clear sense of purpose, we will have triumphed.

IMAGINATION, COMPASSION, AND GRATITUDE

If we have no peace, it is because we have forgotten that we belong to each other.

—MOTHER TERESA

Imagination is also at the heart of happiness. This goes beyond creative imagination, like when you sit down to pen a poem or put watercolors to canvas. The type of imagination refers to imagining yourself in another person's shoes, imagining what someone else is experiencing.

Rowling also had much to say about this, but here's a short snippet: "Unlike any other creature on this planet, humans can learn and understand without having experienced. They can think themselves into other people's places." What a wonderful power! Why live just one life when you can live a thousand and learn from every one of them? Empathy is increased a thousandfold.

Through imagination, we learn to have compassion for our fellow humans. This is a step toward living a compassionate life and toward having compassion for yourself and for others. Compassion and gratitude are paths that lead to happiness.

Through imagination, we learn to have compassion for our fellow humans. This is a big step toward living your life with compassion—for yourself and for others. Compassion and gratitude are paths toward happiness.

BEGINNING YOUR JOURNEY

It is more fun to talk with someone who doesn't use long, difficult words but rather short, easy words like "What about lunch?"

—WINNIE THE POOH

Perhaps the single-most contented and wise creature ever imagined is Winnie the Pooh. The master of Zen and the art of honey-tummy maintenance has forgotten more about being happy than most of us will ever learn. In fact, he forgets nearly everything that isn't related to one of his deep, loving friendships. However, the charming implication in his stories is that he *chooses* to put his challenges into perspective. When reminded of something he has inadvertently mucked up, he will dismiss his mistake with a heartfelt apology. There's much we can all glean from Pooh's implacable calm and goodwill.

Embody some of this calm and goodwill and become an active participant in identifying your life's unique and singular purpose. Like Pooh, when you are happy, you can't help spreading joy to others. There are tools you can grasp that have the potential to make you happier and more purpose-driven every day for the rest of your one and only life.

Pay particular attention to three things:

First, be inspired by the resources we include: TED Talks, films, apps, books, songs, poetry, and quotations.

Second, do some of the practical and fun exercises, either by yourself or with your friends and family. You'll even find one designed with children in mind.

Third, practice what you learn in your daily life.

You are being given tools that will increase your own happiness quotient by leading you to find your life's purpose that you can then live with abundance. By understanding current research and engaging in practical exercises and inspirational reflections, you will live a happier, more joyful, purpose-driven life.

"VI"
Emily Dickinson

If I can stop one heart from breaking,
I shall not live in vain;
If I can ease one life the aching,
Or cool one pain,
Or help one fainting robin
Unto his nest again,
I shall not live in vain.

2

Who Is Happy?

A man sees in the world what he carries in his heart.

—GOETHE

What does a happy person look like? Can we immediately recognize happiness in others? What is the confluence of variables that contribute to a state of happiness?

Each person's smile is unique, but many of the factors that cause the muscles of the face to lift are shared across the entire human family. Happiness, while certainly a subjective state of mind, can be mined for root causes. To some degree, it can be quantified and sourced. A variety of factors influence our feelings of joy, from social status to gender, age, and geography. Some are easy to anticipate—for instance, wealthy people are generally happier than those at the bottom end of the economic ladder.[1] Some are surprising—those of the Jewish faith, with its long history of persecution, are the happiest.[2] Even height plays a role, with taller people being happier than their more petite friends.[3]

In exploring the question, "Who is happiest?" *The New York Times* drew delightful demographic data from the Gallup-

Healthways Well-Being Index. This used a clinical-grade measurement that has for nearly a decade been used to track the main variables. The primary elements that influence happiness are sense of purpose, social relationships, financial security, relationship to community, and physical health. Using these themes, it is possible to create a composite of the happiest person, the one who is at the pinnacle of all these categories.

This exercise is not unlike the technique employed by marketing mavens to identify and study the ideal potential customer. However, the Gallup-Healthways Well-Being Index relied on real people, not idealized composites, and it led to the doorstep of Alvin Wong of Honolulu, Hawaii. Alvin is a five-foot-ten, sixty-nine-year-old Chinese American who is married with children and a Kosher-observing Jewish man. He owns his own business and earns more than $120,000 a year.[4] You could call him the happiest man alive.

The primary elements that influence happiness are sense of purpose, social relationships, financial security, relationship to community, and physical health.

Alvin Wong's high happiness quotient is linked to a dozen factors, but one of them stands out prominently above and beyond all others—he lives in Hawaii. Researchers at the University of Vermont discovered that "happiness rises and falls with distance from the equator." Likewise, *The New York Times* found that living on an island increases happiness.[5] But sunshine alone does not account for the rise of happy feelings in the tropics. Air quality, high-pressure weather systems, and fertile agriculture also help set the scene for serenity and joy. Fresh air from sea breezes bring with it health and vigor. Spending time outside is good for the spirit, and when you live near the equator, you can frolic outdoors all year long, soaking up all that sunshine and Vitamin D.

Beyond this, tropical, equatorial populations are often community minded, family oriented, and in many places even tribal.

A main ingredient of happiness is the ability to spend quality time with friends and family. This may be why Colombia, a poverty-stricken country that has struggled with civil war over a long period, has scored at the top of global happiness ratings for years.[6] Colombians tend to express an attitude of "Relax, the world keeps turning." Such unparalleled acceptance and optimism allows one to heighten the enjoyment of everyday life. Colombian families eat together, cook together while drinking rich Colombian coffee, and visit neighbors together. Often, stew is prepared in pots outdoors and served block-party style.

This combination of a support network, a focus on togetherness, and a positive attitude all come together to make for a happy country no matter the struggles they face. While the

University of Vermont study showed that happier countries were closer to the equator, the World Happiness Report 2016 showed notable exceptions. The countries that topped their list had a culture that focused on health, family, and prosperity for all. These countries—Denmark came first, followed by Switzerland, Iceland, Norway, Finland, Canada, and the Netherlands—demonstrate that there is more than one route to happiness.[7]

The tourism industry of Denmark claims that Danes are content because they stay active every day, have great work-leisure balance, live securely through a welfare state, and enjoy a ruggedly beautiful land that boasts pristine air and water.[8] Rather than hitting the gym to sculpt their bodies, they bike everywhere. They don't call it exercise; they call it "going out." With a thirty-five-hour workweek, going out happens often. With phenomenal social services, there are many public museums, parks, and universities to visit. Lives are lived together, with shared chores, shared cooking, and shared stories. Extended families are as common in Denmark as they are in Mexico and Colombia, where elders pass down long-standing traditions firsthand.

Companionship equals bliss, and even keeping good company with yourself can help lift your mood. Perhaps Americans should learn to love themselves and take better care of themselves. Oprah Winfrey was really onto something when she said, "Your life is a journey to love yourself first and then extending that love to others in every encounter." Taking a warm bath with dozens of candles is a common luxury in Denmark. So is wrapping Christmas presents together with a dozen cousins. The pursuit of good feelings is so central to Danish life that they have a word for it: *hygge*.

Pronounced "hue-gah," this Danish tradition calls for warm, snuggly feelings, and anything that can contribute to those feelings is highly valued. It is the mind-set of taking ordinary everyday tasks and making them special. Fireplaces, hot chocolate, flannel blankets, and warm socks are hygge. Visiting your grandmother and learning about family traditions from her is hygge. Sharing Grandma's cookies with coworkers is oh so hygge. Bringing coworkers to your children's piano recital is hygge. It is the essence of warm, joyful camaraderie, and it brings the man-made sunshine of happiness to these places where real sunshine only exists half of the year.[9]

Hygge is important to the study of happiness because it represents an active cultural focus on the importance of feeling happy. Much like the Colombian attitude of *tranquilo* ("Relax, man!"), the Danish hygge embodies a cultural attitude that puts optimism at the forefront. It is written into these societies that happiness is something to be sought after, and the very act of seeking contentment is sufficiently important to assign a word to it. Children are taught to see the world as a place to experience joy and are taught that joy must be shared with others. In sum, hygge is a *charmed*, *cozy* experience that leads to *contentment*.

The 2016 World Happiness Report examined six core factors: GDP per capita, social support, life expectancy, freedom to make life choices, generosity, and freedom from corruption. Not having basic needs met has a deleterious effect on happiness. It is difficult to be cheerful when corruption in government affects the basic elements of your life, right?

Whereas happiness-paragon Alvin Wong makes over $120,000 each year and lives in a peaceful environment, the average income for Burundi, the lowest country on the 2016 World Happiness Report, is only $770. Nigerians make $938 per year, and Niger is near the bottom of the happiness well. In general, the African countries on the low end of the index share two common traits: they are extremely poor, and they live in continual violent rebellion.[10]

Oprah Winfrey was really onto something when she said, "Your life is a journey to love yourself first and then extending that love to others in every encounter."

Suffering and conflict alone will not crush joy, however. That is clear across many cultures and many eras of time. Colombians have lived in constant danger through decades-long civil war and drug trafficking, but they enjoy dancing, drinking coffee with friends, festive celebrations, and church.

People of the Jewish faith have been persecuted for centuries, and yet Jews are the happiest of the religious sects. Jewish suffering has led to closeness with others who have a shared experience, even if they are strangers across the globe. To build on this vital connection, Israel offers a free visit to any Jewish museum.

Mormons are also ranked highly on the happiness scale, with their weekly tradition of Family Home Evenings, a focus on family, and an ever-expanding circle of supportive friends. It could very well be that poor, war-torn countries score lowest on the index because many have lost family members, have no support from governments, and generally lack a cultural environment to safely enjoy time with friends and loved ones.

Regardless, across all countries, the four most palpable behaviors of happy *cultures* are to stay active, appreciate nature, take a break from television and smartphones, and, most importantly, spend time with friends and family.[11]

AGE

Even if I knew that tomorrow the world would go to pieces, I would still plant my apple tree.

—MARTIN LUTHER

Over the years, the relationship between happiness and age has shown a positive correlation—that is, the older one gets, the more cheerful one's outlook on life. Some studies disagree, showing some muddled data regarding those on the elder end of the spectrum, but overall, old age brings joy more often than misery.

In 2010, an experiment was published that further identified the correlation between joy and age. Arthur Stone of the Department of Psychiatry at Stony Brook University analyzed a Gallup survey of more than 340,000 adults living in the United States. At the time, these participants were between the ages of eighteen and eighty-five, allowing for a wide range of attitude differences. The survey found that those young and old both had higher levels of bliss than did those in the midrange ages. Those between ages twenty-two and twenty-five reported the highest stress levels but also experienced a relatively high degree of happiness. Stress levels dropped sharply after age fifty. Young adults between eighteen and twenty-two were reportedly as happy as people in their seventies and eighties.

Basically, the young and idealistic were happy—that is, once the moodiness of the teen years wore off. As their hormones waned, mood swings subsided and depression was less common. Then, as retirement age rolled around, participants were once again happy.[12]

The reason those who were older exhibited greater joy is that they have greater control of emotions and a breadth of experience that can only accompany maturity. The trials of life are mostly behind those of advanced age, for better or worse, and with that there is twenty-twenty hindsight. As hindsight provides clarity, perspective increases as does the capacity for gratitude. With age, we find it easier to be thankful for what we have in our life, because we have known hardship. We have experienced what it means when the good things in our life fall away, often unexpectedly. Those who are older also are more inclined to share their experiences and their gratitude with their family and friends.

While we know that the older one gets, the happier one tends to be, there are exceptions. There are those who experience isolation and loneliness. At a nursing home in Seattle, the elderly were paired with preschool children. Five days a week, they came together for shared activities that included dancing, art, music, and storytelling. It was reported that the nursing home residents were completely transformed by the children. They became happier and more alive.[13] This interaction with youth and the joy that ensued was an antidote to loneliness.

But some conflict exists when it comes to research on whether most grow happier with age. There is conflicting research about the smiling propensity of the elderly. In studies comparing middle-aged adults and older adults, the older ones at times have been found to be *less* happy. This wrinkle was resolved in a 2013 paper, which found that the period when a person is born can affect their level of joy for all their lives.

After controlling for such variables as wealth, gender, ethnicity, and education, it was established that happiness increases over everyone's lifetime. No matter who you are, you will get happier as you age with one exception. People who started life during a difficult period like the Great Depression had a more challenging time achieving bliss. At age seventy, those who lived through the Great Depression were not as happy as those born earlier or later.

Interestingly, there is some recent evidence that the age-equals-happy formula is evolving or breaking down. While middle-aged people have sometimes been found to be happier than younger adults, they are now less happy than they used to be. According to Jean Twenge and her colleagues, thirty-somethings today are significantly unhappier than thirty-somethings twenty years ago. Sifting through data from 1972 to 2014 from four national samples totaling 1.3 million participants, Twenge discovered that old age is still a blissful destination, but it can be hard getting there.

Middle-aged adults today are less happy than their predecessors, likely because of a disparity between expectations and what reality is dishing up. And this trend may continue. The data showed that 64 percent of 2015's high school grads expect to become a successful professional or a manager of a business. That is up from 48 percent in 1976. However, the actual percentage of people getting those positions is still 18 percent, as it has been since the 1970s. So today's youth are more optimistic, happy, and inspired, and then they grow up and try to get jobs in their late twenties and thirties. Suddenly, reality strikes hard, and they hit the low levels of contentment found in the mid-age range.[14]

This is becoming a prevalent concern, as past research has shown that happiness is lower when income inequality is greater. Young adult and teens do not feel the difference in pay as much, since they have only just begun working and don't expect to make that much money . . . right now. After ten years and dwindling hope, though, the future for many will be less bright.

Jean Twenge points out another factor in the middle-age happy dip: the rise of individualism. Individualism is a cultural emphasis on the self and a weakening of traditional social rules. This is great for young people, who are still finding themselves and do not wish to be bound by traditional values, rules, or relationships. However, when these individuals who have struck out on their own reach middle age, they may find themselves wishing they had a community of support.

And the data confirm what has been shown elsewhere about the elderly. As they age, they can often become isolated because of the death of peers or a spouse. This loss of friends and family has been proven repeatedly to be the foundation of limiting enduring happiness.

Hygge is important to the study of happiness because it represents an active cultural focus on feeling happy. Much like the Colombian attitude of tranquilo ("Relax, man!"), the Danish *hygge* embodies a cultural attitude that puts optimism in the forefront. This Danish tradition is the mind-set of taking ordinary everyday tasks and making them special; it is a charmed, cozy experience that leads to contentment.

POLITICS

Happiness is found by those who truly engage with life, and it is boosted by interacting with and participating in activities that increase social connectivity. Both factors align with political engagement as a path to happiness. Politics can be tremendously rewarding as you consider ways to order your society, give back to others, and live a life of purpose.

A fascinating study published in 2011 in the *Journal of Public Deliberation* by a pair of researchers at the University of Wollongong in Australia made some very bold claims.[15] These authors asserted that social participation is "the happiness connection." The study focused on three areas of daily life where we have the power to influence outcomes through day-to-day decisions: personal relationships, work, and citizenship. It then explored how these areas correlate to ratings of overall happiness. In terms of time invested, because we spend most of the hours of our lives with our families and in the workplace, how we feel during those hours hugely contributes to how happy we generally feel. These authors took that common-sense understanding a step further and tested this hypothesis: whether experiencing greater democracy in the family and in the workplace may lead to greater happiness.

A mountain of previously published research studies shows that decision-making strongly correlates to happiness levels. An implication of this that naturally stands out is that changing one's thoughts, habits, and behaviors is the most effective way to escalate your happiness quotient. When we distill the ingredients in the recipe to cook up happiness, we find that the essential ingredient—the saffron of happiness—is our pattern of thoughts.

As researchers Chris Barker and Brian Martin aptly wrote in their assessment of what most correlates to happiness, "Happiness depends more on patterns of thinking than upon actual events. The implication is to deliberately cultivate particular ways of thinking, including fostering forgiveness and gratitude about the past, savouring the present moment, and looking to the future with hope and optimism."

For many, discussions of politics conjure up conflict, debate, and division. But politics is also about building relationships, a commitment to service, and, in the best sense, it's about altruism—doing for others and creating a better world. Social and political participation can provide one's life with a sense of meaning. And we know that having meaning in one's life is a threshold to happiness.

We can make a case for participating in the helter-skelter political process as one way to provide people with a sense of meaning in their lives. Research has well established this as a way to find a life of purpose. The most accessible and obvious form of citizen participation in the political process is voting. Several studies on South American, Canadian, and Swiss voting behavior have shown that people who turn out to vote in an election report greater life satisfaction than those who do not. There's evidence that it's not actually the vote itself that matters but rather the opportunity to vote—the choice one makes to determine the outcome of issues in their community. Viewing the outcome of nation-states that transform from a nondemocratic government to a democracy only serve to corroborate this fact.

When we distill the ingredients in the recipe to cook up happiness, we find that the essential ingredient— the saffron of happiness—is our pattern of thoughts.

It's important to remember, however, that voting is just an occasional event. There are many ways you can contribute. If you want to influence what appears on the ballot, you can get involved in a deeper way. Being involved in the political process can readily take the form of participating in an electoral campaign. You may opt to participate in public meetings, raise money in support of a candidate, throw your weight behind an issue, organize a protest, write letters to newspaper editors, pen opinion articles for the media. You may want to join other citizens and canvass door-to-door. These are all activities that will demonstrate your influence and contribute to a life of purpose.

There are other leadership activities to consider. Become a member of your local town meeting committee or advocate for an initiative, petition, or referendum.

From this framework, the two Australian researchers answered two important questions: If people choose to participate in politics, does that make them happier? Do happier people participate more?

If happiness is positively correlated with relationships, as we know that it is, then it stands to reason that civic participation, by building relationships, may also contribute to happiness. It's true. Civic involvement forms and extends relationships beyond family, friends, and leisure-time connections. Ongoing interactions with others related to issues of mutual interest are likely to enhance your sense of personal satisfaction. It is exciting to be among those who rally around an issue or political candidate because they are doing it to create what they believe to be a better world, and there is no better contribution to society.

Political engagement is its own reward. Feeling like your actions made a difference or helped those in need is tremendously rewarding to others and to yourself. There are many issues through which you can engage—support of greater diversity, support for improved living and of working conditions, and support for health care and education for all. A prime example of a rewarding effort is being a peace worker. Creating conditions that will foster peace have far-reaching ripple effects. It can help reduce human suffering and enable greater happiness for others both in the present and as a legacy for the future.

So it seems that political engagement can be a path to happiness simply by choosing to participate in the process. But it is interesting to note that there is a self-selection bias in those who choose to participate in the political process. The process makes them happier over time, and happier people participate more. The lesson from all of this is that political participation will make participants even more satisfied and, in turn, even more willing to participate further. It is a self-perpetuating and happy process.

PET OWNERS

Behold the power of pets.

Now, we know that social relationships have a huge influence on well-being. Here's a good question: Does the relationship need to be human? No. As it turns out, social support and a sense of belonging can come from a sweet friend that has four legs, fur, or feathers.

Rigorous social psychology research demonstrates that pet owners score more favorably on numerous mental and physical health measures.[16] Compared to people who do not share their lives with a pet, pet owners have greater self-esteem, are less fearful and lonely, and are more likely to regularly work out and, thus, be physically fit. The pet owners also were found to be supportive parents and siblings and to support family members.

Interestingly, people who are pet owners tend to rate their human relationships as close. Taken together, what this information confirms is that pet lovers are socially skillful people and more extroverted than average. They have big hearts and bestow good feelings on both animals and people. Having a pet does not replace a human social network but rather enhances and enlarges it. Cats, dogs, birds—and pets of all species, shapes, and sizes—bring wellness.

Under controlled lab conditions, the study also revealed

that pets inoculate people against the effects of social rejection. Writing about their pets made people less susceptible to feeling low after being rejected as compared to a control group. It was also found that in this regard, the pet friend and the human friend were just as effective as a means of providing social support. The bottom line for these researchers was that pets infuse substantial well-being benefits to their humans.

People tend to associate themselves into one of two categories when it comes to pets: either they are a "cat person" or a "dog person." Some people pledge their allegiance to both camps. There's even pet rivalry. Some say that dogs are better than cats (or vice versa). Is there a basis for this?

Do dog people really differ from cat people?

This question was asked of more than 250 adults in the United States by researchers at New York's Manhattanville College. One of the findings is that pet owners have a higher life satisfaction score than individuals who chose to not share life with a pet.[17]

The study also found that dog and cat owners showed significant psychological differences. Dog owners tended to score higher on psychological tests of well-being, with higher scores specifically for being more conscientious and less neurotic. It was also found that dog owners are more extroverted and generally more agreeable.

The researchers note that "personality likely influences our choices to adopt a pet and which pet we choose, but our personality is not fixed, so it could also be influenced by our relationships with others, including our pets." The bond between owner and pet is emotional and chemical as well. It turns out that oxytocin is released when we hang out with our four-legged friends.

This study even measured the oxytocin released by the pets themselves. There was evidence to back any dog owner who wants to make the case that dogs love their owners more than cats do. Saliva samples taken from dogs and cats after ten minutes of play with their owners revealed that oxytocin surges five times higher for dogs than for cats.

Studies have also shown that dog owners are less likely to have depression. Caring for a dog can help build greater resilience and coping skills to ward off depression, anxiety, and dangerous levels of stress. The American Heart Association has found a link between owning a pet—especially a dog—and reduced risk of hypertension and stroke, as well as a longer life span with fewer visits to the doctor over the years.[18] Go, Fido!

MONEY

There is a time-honored adage that says that having it all is believing that you do. Modern research on the relationship between material wealth and happiness gives this a full-on and ringing endorsement.

Counterintuitive to the cultural message that being rich is the secret to a good life, studies have shown that the relationship between money and happiness is surprisingly weak. Part of the problem in studying this issue is that money and financial security correlate with other factors contributing to happiness, such as free time, health, and travel.

These correlations are not causal, meaning that while happiness and wealth may coexist, cash is not necessarily what led to happiness. For example, healthier people will be content with or without money and will also be more capable of earning money. While it can be said that money leads to happiness through purchasing power, the actual effect of currency on life is a challenge to quantify.

Some people assert that making money isn't the point of life, whereas others say financial security is the primary reason they work. In fact, most people say that increased cash would alleviate their current woes.[19] So it seems that money can't buy you happiness, but it can purchase a relief from stress.

There is a time-honored adage that says having it all is believing that you already do.

In the 1970s and 1980s, it was commonly believed by psychologists that there was no relationship between money and happiness. One 1978 study on lottery winners and accident victims found that winning the lottery *decreased* participants' enjoyment of simple, mundane tasks and that their subjective happiness was no different from that of the control group. Meanwhile, people who had been paralyzed by auto accidents reported more satisfaction with daily life than lottery winners.[20]

Data gathered over the years has amounted to cash flow information on hundreds of thousands of people in over 150 countries. The surveys show that overall, richer people are happier with their lot in life and have fewer stressors. However, this effect is only salient to a certain threshold. The exact figure changes depending on the cost of living, but for Americans, the magic yearly income is around $40,000–50,000. Above this amount, the effect of cash on being happy is slightly higher but is relatively miniscule.

One study indicated that a doubling of income is necessary to experience even a small boost of contentment. Likewise, even though there is only a minor impact on happiness, more money does continue to increase capacity for pleasure, with no upper limit. This point is particularly apparent in wealthy developed countries where there are more things to buy.

When people were asked whether they were happy *right now*, the effect of money was extremely negligible. In one large study, sifting through survey data from all over the world, it was found that participants self-reported similar happiness levels whether they were earning $2,000 a year or $32,000.[21]

What does this mean for one's personal pursuit of happiness? It means that a rough happiness goal for income should be about $40,000 for a single person living in the United States. More is necessary if you have children or other dependents or if you live in New York City, but shooting for that threshold should maximize the joy return on one's income.[22] Above that number, satisfaction through money is based on other factors, such as purchasing life experiences or increasing your social footprint through philanthropy and charitable work.

Seeking interesting experiences and adventures is a great way to increase one's quality of life. It is a great way to enhance the mood return on investment for money spent. When we simply buy things, we make ourselves happy in the moment, but the thrill is temporary; it eventually wears off. To have a permanent effect, one would need to continue replenishing by buying new things—or perhaps find another strategy that will lead to lasting happiness.

In contrast, purchasing a trip or a language lesson will create a lasting sense of accomplishment and joy. If you spend money on bettering yourself and expanding your life experience, you reap the rewards forever. A new TV will need to be upgraded every few years, but the memories of being in a gondola on the Grand Canal in Venice will offer memories to savor and and carry with you throughout your life.[23] Joy is found by savoring your experiences, what the poet John Keats called "moments big as years."

That's not to say retail therapy doesn't work. Anyone who knows the joy of finding a magnificent bargain or who has carried brightly wrapped packages in one hand and a peppermint mocha in the other knows the pleasure that shopping can offer. Researchers at the University of Michigan confirm the satisfaction found in retail therapy. Their research showed that shopping can reduce sadness by reducing a subjective sense of powerlessness. Buying something can restore your sense of control over your life.[24]

A 2011 experiment supported this data, indicating that strategic self-treating with shopping can be a motivator for performance, which can in turn lead to satisfaction with one-self. In this way, money is a creator of happiness; cash enables you to buy something and encourages you to become a better person, which then makes you happy with yourself. It is important to note that most of the positive effects of retail therapy stem from the fact that shopping is making us happier with ourselves. It's not about the things.

Money also can enable dressing for success. This can affect mental performance as well as social appearance. Take the following examples. In one study, people accurately judged a person's attitude, gender, age, and income just from pictures of his or her shoes. Now who says women often have too many shoes? Another study examined the impact of purchasing clothing related to your job or role. It found that participants did better on a series of lab tasks when wearing newly purchased lab coats than they did when wearing street clothes.[25]

Philanthropy is another good way to increase self-satisfaction and help others achieve more happiness from their own income. Thích Nhất Hạnh once said, "Compassion is a verb." How we would all thrive so much more if we learned to be actively compassionate—for ourselves as much as for others.

Elizabeth Dunn of the University of British Colombia studies giving and conducts experiments to teach people how to help themselves by helping others. Dunn gives people money and then instructs them either to spend it on themselves or to spend it on someone else. Those that bought for others reported significantly higher levels of satisfaction with their purchases.[26]

Giving money to charity is also a way to buy life experiences for yourself. Charitable donations create an endorphin effect in the brain like that of sex and chocolate. Using fMRI technology, researchers watched the midbrain light up when people donated to a worthy cause.[27] What comprises a worthy cause? Data from around the world indicate that those living with a $1,000 yearly income would feel a much greater effect from donations than would someone earning $10,000. Since we know that income directly influences happiness up to about $40,000 a year, international donations to developing countries will have an exponentially greater benefit on the human condition.

BEAUTY

Naomi Wolf, author of *The Beauty Myth*, said that capitalism and male dominance have created the concept of beauty for cultural consumption. She maintains that consumer magazines advertise popular beauty images to stir up envy and desire. This helps them achieve power through money and by sidelining women in roles as models and those who are wannabe models.[28]

But this is not the entire picture, since Wolf presented this message in 1991, and, as we know, Renaissance art fully displayed flesh and lace hundreds of years prior. Of course, those plump figures reclining in Italian oil paintings are a far cry from the rail-thin models of the '60s and even from today's severe and angular supermodels.

This only shows that evaluating beauty and bliss is tricky business. We live in what Nancy Etcoff calls "an age of ugly beauty." In her book *Survival of the Prettiest*, she asserts that today traditional beauty is viewed with suspicion and malice in society, and ugliness has gained traction as a new form of beauty. Thick-rimmed black glasses and square-cut dresses flourish in expensive boutiques, and cheerleaders are at times portrayed as the mean girls of pop culture. Yet cheerleaders are still homecoming queens, and *Playboy* still recruits conventional beauties for its pages. This means that the average person experiences a wide range of conflicting emotions about appearances.

The upshot of this ambiguity is that almost any psychological mind-set can be created as it relates to the correlation of beauty to personal happiness. Some may find the pursuit of beauty satisfying while others may find *being* beautiful a powerful source of comfort. Yet some *strive* to be ugly to differentiate themselves from the crowd.

Beauty is a vague but primal concept that somehow manages to drive a huge portion of our activities. Saying that beauty is in the eye of the beholder essentially makes the claim that beauty is undefinable. That is hard to believe, considering that beauty products and services are a multibillion-dollar industry. The beauty purveyors have an idea of what beauty is. Hair care alone provided $11.8 billion in revenue in 2015.[29]

It has been notoriously difficult to pinpoint the appeal of attractiveness and to avoid falling into a variety of psychological traps when assessing beauty. There's a halo effect to beauty. Strangers think more positively of attractive people and of their abilities, assuming they have intelligence or kindness. It is consistently shown, however, that being attractive, whatever the definition may be, is positively correlated with happiness.

For example, tall people have been shown to have greater satisfaction with their lives than short people.[30] The impact of height diminishes when the person has greater mental ability or financial security, but other aspects of appearance continue to influence happiness. A 2016 study in the *Journal of Happiness Studies* showed a significant positive relationship between physical attractiveness and psychological well-being. This study followed participants from teenage years through adulthood. During high school, greater facial attractiveness was conducive to happiness, and in middle age, lower BMI made folks happy. Additionally, a lower self-perception of physical beauty was found to create distress and depression.[31] So, beauty isn't just good for making you happy, it can also keep you from being sad.

Attractiveness itself has a quantifiable value. Viewing beautiful faces alone can create a reward reaction in the brain, even without any anticipation of interaction with the pretty or handsome subject. Indeed, assessing the subjects' level of attractiveness was an independent reaction.[32] In other words, people gain reward from viewing pretty people. It just happens.

What does this mean for personal happiness? If one strives to be attractive, it enhances the lives of others through passive rewards. People see you and become happier themselves. This in turn can be a great source of joy for the one who has put effort and time into looking good. Social reward systems are powerful, and it is gratifying to be a source of happiness.

Lastly, as with many happiness factors, appearances can be deceiving. Many studies have shown a connection between attraction and healthy attributes, such as rosy skin, firm muscles, and alert eyes. Since health is always a top indicator of happiness, there is a strong chance that people with low BMI and tight skin are content in great part because they are hale and hearty.

GENDER

Women and men each have strong opinions on who is the happier gender. Or perhaps more accurately, they have strong opinions on who is the moodier, angrier, and grouchier gender. Conflicting research shows that happiness measures are different for men and women, and the jury is out on which gender is happiest.

The World Happiness Report 2016 stated that men are happier than women.[33] A study in 2013 found that women are happier than men—but 64 percent of women *thought* men were happier. Yet another survey showed that gender happiness switches as age sets in.

An analysis in the *Journal of Happiness Studies* involving forty-seven thousand people in America assessed happiness through self-reporting. Researchers found that young women are happier than young men, and that the gap closes with age. By age forty-eight, men pass women on the blissful scale. Young men reportedly have poor love lives, compared to what they want or need, and low-paying jobs when culture dictates that they must earn a significant income. By later life, they are married and have secure jobs and income, offering them a state of contentment.

Women, on the other hand, start off with advantages in maturity and prospects. In addition, being attractive can be a premium asset for women, but less so for men. Youthful beauty is on the girls' side. As they near that forty-eight-year mark, though, some have fewer prospects and may have ostensibly lost a primary advantage over men.[34] Anecdotally, some women dispute these findings, reporting that later in life they are more confident, have had professional success, and, thus, a variety of exciting life experiences.

The prospect of marriage is one area where joy can come and go. Peggy Drexler, psychologist and author, says that the prevalence of divorce in modern times is not a sign of the breakdown of happiness but rather "evidence of the long, slow decline of expectations."[35] Society no longer dictates that couples remain married forever. Women are also more likely to be self-supporting and independent, with money and time to pursue their own happiness. Changing cultural expectations have set both genders free from the cage of expected marriage until death. Now that we live longer, we have more time to be happy.

Although women are now financially able to leave a marriage or pursue nontraditional lifestyles, it hasn't automatically translated into greater reports of happiness. Conversely, women in conservative roles like mother, housewife, and teacher report more joy than their liberated sisters. This might be because women in liberal areas notice discrimination because they compare their salaries and opportunities to everyone else of both genders, whereas traditional women may focus their identities around traditional gender roles, meaning they compare themselves to other women without including men.[36]

Additionally, since women have made gains in rights in recent decades, mundane chores and the trappings of lifestyles common to earlier generations can annoy them. For example, men who do household chores report feeling happier because of it, often because there is no expectation that it is a requirement of their role. They gain enjoyment from being open-minded, agreeable, helpful mates. Women, on the other hand, can feel shoehorned into a traditional role and taken advantage of when they are expected to do the dishes. This subjective measure of contentment is similar to the effect of wage inequality in general, where people are gloomier when they can see others getting more than they do.[37] What this emphasizes again is the trigger expectations can have on happiness and contentment.

Studies that show women who are happier than men credit this to women's social outlook. The secret to a positive outlook is proven to be social interaction and a focus on family and friends. While men are more likely to gain pleasure from hobbies and personal achievements, women derive more joy from making other people happy.

According to surveys, 54 percent of women say they strive to make others happy, and 76 percent say that doing so makes them feel good. These numbers far outpace men's responses and likely lead to stronger social networks as they help others find joy. In addition, 62 percent of women feel a greater sense of well-being when they see others laugh or smile, compared to 56 percent of men.[38] The feedback loop of making others happy and thereby making oneself happy could be an area of discovery for future happiness research.

RELIGION

People may sing in church, but does religion really make one happier? Research is highly dependent upon where data are collected, but overall, there seems to be a tie between who is happier, those who are religious or those who are atheists. What is known is that there is no significant difference between the two. Those with an open-minded, general spirituality are also in the mix, and though they score lower in most studies on joy, their positive spirituality of beliefs is probably the number-one contribution religion makes to their sense of well-being.

Edward Diener of Harvard University has been studying religion's effect on bliss for more than a decade. Data are unclear in pointing to a direct path to happiness, indicating that not all religious people are happy, not all religious happiness levels are the same, and not all religious beliefs lead to happiness. With the variance in these results, it is important to search for the one element of religion that brings the contentment most often expressed by many who identify as faithful. Diener argues that "one key ingredient is positive spirituality, feeling emotions such as love, awe, wonder, respect, and gratitude that connect us to others and to things larger than ourselves."[39]

To those who study happiness, this is no surprise. Connections with family, friends, and community are at the very top of every conclusion on the catalysts of contentment. Religion often offers people social support and human contact, providing a safety net that may not be present outside of church. At places of worship, people can meet other like-minded people and sometimes must count on those folks for help. Minimally, religious gatherings are one valuable way to meet new friends.

Another way religion can bring comfort to practitioners is through the security and optimism of offering an afterlife. Death is a frightening concept for most people, and religions offer explanations of what happens when we breathe our last breath. Whether they are right or not doesn't matter so much, as they hold out a belief for those who wish to grasp it. This ability to explain death is a central contributor to bliss for those who choose to accept it.

Religion provides a moral compass to those who are not able to craft one themselves. It offers rules to live by for those who lack the personal experience to independently decide between right and wrong. The concept of right and wrong is explained by all faiths and is valuable particularly when cultural norms may conflict with instinctual inclinations.

Some things need explaining, and even if they do not make sense when viewed from another's culture and perspective, it is important to remember that most people seek to live a stress-free life among their peers. Religion serves up just that—a series of right and wrong, good and bad, to make navigating through life just that much easier for those who choose it.

For many people, planning and decision-making are stressful and terrifying. The daily practice of deciding what to do—how to react to hostile coworkers, when to give back a lost wallet and when to use the found money to save a child—are overwhelming without a guiding philosophy. Likewise, the social judgment associated with making a "wrong" choice in the eyes of your community can be difficult to bear, and it is often easier to go with the flow and simply do what others are doing. Since religion provides specific rules for just about everything, religion provides a clear rule book.

Not everyone follows rule books written by others. Individual spirituality can be as satisfying as organized religion, and even atheism can offer happiness. However, much of the current research implies that it is the commitment to a philosophy that creates the sense of well-being associated with religion, not the doctrine.

One study in *Psychological Medicine* followed over eight thousand people in both rural and urban areas in seven countries for one year. Examined twice during that year, the participants reported on such things as current happiness levels, whether they had become depressed within the time period, and how they identified their religious beliefs. It was found that those most likely to be depressed were those without a strict religion. Indeed, only 10.5 percent of people with a "general spiritual understanding of life" became depressed. Religious folks were close behind, however, with a mere 10.3 percent becoming depressed. Interestingly, only 7 percent of atheists reported being depressed.[40]

In a larger 2016 World Happiness Report survey that evaluated religions across the world, extremely religious Jews were found to have the highest levels of contentment. Almost as happy were Mormons and atheists, a fact that certainly confounds any attempts to say that belief in a god is the magic ingredient for happiness in religion. Catholics and Protestants followed.[41]

If this looks like a guide to choosing the religion that will make you happiest, remember that data can be deceptive. The World Happiness Report controlled for many factors, but one thing that was found consistently was that those who practiced religion were happier the more they practiced it—that is, if you are religious, it is best to go all in and be as active as possible in your church community. Levels of happiness were always correlated with levels of personal religiosity, a fact that has been supported in other studies, even those conducted by atheists.

Jochen Gebauer of Humboldt University in Berlin and

Constantine Sedikides of the University of Southampton (UK) created a study to estimate individual psychological adjustment relative to the surrounding religious fervor in a handful of countries. Psychological adjustment was based on self-assessment of how well one could adapt and endure, as well as his or her ability to be cheerful and optimistic. They also estimated social self-esteem drawn from self-reported responses to social situations and how easy it was to make new friends.

The results showed a strong correlation between personal religiosity and the country of residence. Additionally, the study found that while religious people were happier in religious countries, nonreligious people were unhappier. This is likely due to the good feelings that come with belonging to a large group and knowing that others in society think and feel the way you do.

Religious people were also happy in secular countries, though secular people were very unhappy in religious places. A conclusion is that secular places make everyone welcome, while religious places are dependent on uniformity to provide happiness. In other words, one can be a Christian in Denmark or Sweden, but it is difficult to be an atheist in Turkey, Iran, or America.[42]

Being mainstream is comforting, but this isn't the whole picture. It is the comfort of knowing life, and afterlife, will be taken care of that creates comfort and happiness in people. Residents of highly socially developed countries have less need for religion and church support because they can provide it for themselves or their government will provide it. There is no fear of facing old age in extreme poverty. Danes and Swedes are confident in their own welfare and do not need to turn to prayer to provide hope for their future. Taxes do that.[43]

This is further supported by some data from the United States. The most religious states are the least happy, based on Gallup polls. They also have the lowest levels of civil services, such as schools and emergency services. This could explain why the United States is more religious than Europe despite having a similar level of economic development.

In the end, what religion offers can be found in any religious choice, even choosing not to have a religion. Whatever the personal choice, there is the comfort of having a rule book to live life by, the physical security provided by a community of supportive peers, and time spent with friends and family that create happiness in church, synagogue, temple, or coffeehouse.

PROFESSION

We all spend a significant chunk of our life, hours, and days working. Therefore, we have hopefully chosen employment that makes us feel happy and fulfilled. Attaining happiness at work is possible; it is a choice. But what career you choose appears to relate to your overall level of happiness.

The top-five happiest professions in recent years have been those of software developer, computer network architect, construction manager, facility manager, and database administrator. The factors that contribute to a sense of happiness at work are feeling challenged, having variety and autonomy, doing immersive tasks, and making others happy.[44]

Teachers also were among those who "rate their lives better than all other occupational groups, except for physicians. Specifically, teachers scored higher than almost all occupational groups, including executives, nurses, construction workers and business owners on life evaluations, plus four areas of well-being: emotional health, healthy behaviors, basic access and physical health."[45]

In contrast, some of the unhappiest jobs in the country include sales account manager and security officer.[46] Sales managers work in a fiercely competitive environment and manage teams of individuals who by virtue of the nature of their jobs cannot work collaboratively.

Even among jobs where there is greater status, interestingly, there can be an inverse relationship between happiness and prestige or salary. An interesting example is that lowest-paid lawyers are among the happiest![47] These individuals who work for public good spend less time jockeying for position among private law firms.

CEOs are among the most accomplished individuals in the workforce. They generally command handsome salaries and bonuses and enjoy a variety of perks. Given this professional success, one would imagine that most CEOs are driven by a strong sense of purpose. Nick Craig and Scott Snook in a seminal article published in *Harvard Business Review* report that fewer than 20 percent of leaders have identified their individual purpose and fewer still can articulate it into a clear statement.

It is well known that purpose not only brings happiness but also has been found to be the catalyst for exceptional performance. Craig and Snook propose that CEOs who identify their purpose can significantly accelerate their growth and deepen their impact. The value of articulating and living your purpose is proving to be the source of professional success, but it goes far beyond this and can serve as the wellspring of lasting happiness.

You might not be a CEO, but you go to work every day. Do you consider your work a job, a career, or a calling? Let's reflect on the difference. If you consider your work a *job*, your motivation is to pay the bills, and often you may muddle through or think of it as a chore. If you answered *career*, you enjoy your day-to-day efforts and see your work on a trajectory for professional advancement. A *calling*, on the other hand, is a siren song to find meaning and to contribute to the lives of others in the process. Which of the three do you think brings the greatest happiness?

Time published an article a few years ago on how to be happier at work.[48] They focused on the top-five behaviors shown by research to drive happiness in the workplace.

- Start the day off on a positive note.
- Reduce the number of decisions you make.
- Help your colleagues and others.
- Push toward new levels and acknowledge your progress.
- End each day with a statement of gratitude.

There are actionable things we can do every day to be happier. It's one more example of how feeling good is a choice. Let's all choose happy.

"Happiness"
Jane Kenyon

There's just no accounting for happiness,
or the way it turns up like a prodigal
who comes back to the dust at your feet
having squandered a fortune far away.

And how can you not forgive?
You make a feast in honor of what
was lost, and take from its place the finest
garment, which you saved for an occasion
you could not imagine, and you weep night and day
to know that you were not abandoned,
that happiness saved its most extreme form
for you alone.

No, happiness is the uncle you never
knew about, who flies a single-engine plane
onto the grassy landing strip, hitchhikes
into town, and inquires at every door
until he finds you asleep midafternoon
as you so often are during the unmerciful
hours of your despair.

It comes to the monk in his cell.
It comes to the woman sweeping the street
with a birch broom, to the child

whose mother has passed out from drink.
It comes to the lover, to the dog chewing
a sock, to the pusher, to the basketmaker,
and to the clerk stacking cans of carrots
in the night.

It even comes to the boulder
in the perpetual shade of pine barrens,
to rain falling on the open sea,
to the wineglass, weary of holding wine.

3

The Scientific Underpinnings

*Buddha was asked this question: "What have you gained
from meditation?"*
 He replied, "Nothing at all."
 "Then Blessed One, what good is it?"
 *"Let me tell you what I lost through meditation:
sickness, anger, depression, insecurity, the burden of old
age, the fear of death. That is the good of meditation,
which leads to nirvana."*

Some people think of happiness as an art, some think of it
as a life philosophy, while others think of it as a practice.
This is certainly all true, but there is one more fundamental
truth: steps can be taken to intuitively or deliberatively navigate your way to a happy life.

We know this because there is an abundance of evidence
showing that the path to happiness is discoverable through scientific research. We know with certainty that the art, philosophy, and practice of happiness have biomedical underpinnings
and that a life abounding with purpose is a life brimming with

happiness. And there is substantial scientific research to explain exactly why this is so.

There is a robust body of research on the value of cultivating a life of purpose. Thankfully, scientists take this topic seriously and are invested in broadening our understanding of the process and outcomes. This progression of knowledge has been decades in the making.

THE SCIENCE OF HAPPINESS EMERGES

It is not common knowledge that the field of psychology wandered down some alternative paths. Initially, they pointed to the possibility that there is limited human capacity for joy. Two of the most prominent psychologists of the last century were Sigmund Freud and B. F. Skinner. Freud built his legacy on the study of lust and neurosis. His focus on the human personality and its drivers explored the anxiety that arose from basic human needs being unmet. For years, his influence resonated with psychiatrists and psychologists as they focused on the more animalistic and base aspects of the human condition. As they saw it at the time, what drove behavior was always something that was lacking, a worry, an itch that required scratching. Little consideration was given to joy, contentment, and altruism.

The next major psychology doctrine emanated with Skinner and his school of study. It was coined *behaviorism*. Behaviorism is a way of viewing the world with unfeeling billiard-ball logic: *this* happens and then *that* follows. Antecedent and consequence. Stimulus and behavior. Explaining *why* a person engaged in a specific behavior was superfluous and irrelevant to Skinner. He worshiped at the altar of stimulus and response. In behaviorism, hungry bellies get filled and itches get scratched. Purpose is irrelevant. There is no room for talking about curiosity, gratification, or reasoning. There is no room for joy.

Interestingly, behaviorism inadvertently led to an opposite theory, a study initiated by a young operant conditioning researcher named Martin Seligman. Seligman focused on how organisms learn to avoid punishment. The research design was rather grim. A dog would be placed in an experimental room where the floor had a metal grid through which electric shocks could be delivered. The stimulus of a light turning on or a specific sound could predict that the shock was about to begin. During a training period, some dogs could escape the shock by hopping over a barrier to a part of the chamber that did not have the metal grid that delivered a shock. Other dogs were blocked from escape and forced to endure the shocks. Over time, a pattern of behavior called *learned helplessness* was discovered—the dogs that had no choice but to endure the shocks learned to be helpless. When the barrier to safety was later removed and the dogs had the ability to escape the electrical shock, they didn't bother. They had been broken.

This observation led Martin Seligman to plot the opposite trajectory of behaviorism, one that theorized and demonstrated the value of hope, resilience, and a life of purpose. Surprisingly, perhaps, given how his research began, Seligman eventually garnered recognition as the father of positive psychology, the science of what makes people flourish.[1,2] Positive psychology is the rigorous study of strengths, fulfillment, and how to enhance what is positive in life.

Ironically, from the entrails of this dire experiment that extoled pain upon dogs came the optimism of positive psychology. Through positive psychology, individuals and communities can learn to thrive and to optimize health and happiness.

What is it that science has revealed about the relationship between happiness and living a life brimming with purpose? So much is known, and all this knowledge can be used as actionable tools to expedite a journey toward purpose.

Finding your personal purpose is the turnkey to finding joy.

Purpose can be defined as meaningful experiences that are unrelated to baubles, expensive toys, and material objects. Science has shown us that our brains are hardwired to feel ongoing pleasure from rich and meaningful experiences, as opposed to dopamine—the pleasure-reward neurotransmitter—that is on a transient *drip-drip-drip* fed by expensive toys, houses, cars, vacations, and all other forms of conspicuous consumption. Dopamine dwindles over time. Like with a drug addiction, we build tolerance and require bigger hits.

But when we have meaningful experiences with other people, our brains reward us with oxytocin. We feel more connected. We create community and feel safe and more deeply nurtured. Friendship, forgiveness, generosity, gratitude, and service create these meaningful experiences. A positive feedback loop is created when we seek more of those connections, more of these experiences that suffuse the brain in oxytocin, the bonding hormone.

When a life is guided by meaningful experiences, there is no chasing; there is only connection. Creating good experiences for others is a sustainable way to make ourselves happy. And when we are happy, we flourish!

THE SET POINT FOR HAPPINESS

Are we genetically predisposed to be happy or sad? Are there limits to one's personal happiness?

Sonja Lyubomirsky, Ken Sheldon, David Schkade, and Martin Seligman have proposed this formula for happiness:

$$H = S + C + V$$

H: Happiness
S: Set point that we inherit
C: Conditions of living
V: Voluntary actions or choices we make

According to this formula, 50 percent of our happiness is predicated by our set point and, surprisingly, only 10 percent is based on our living conditions. The fact is that whether you live in a mansion in Beverly Hills, in the shantytowns of Johannesburg, or the slums of Calcutta, your potential for happiness is pretty much the same, providing that basic necessities such as water and food are taken care of. Remarkably, an astonishing 40 percent of our happiness is the result of voluntary actions and choices that we make every day. That means that we're born with half of our happiness level. The good news is that the other half of our ability to be happy is fully under our control.

There are some who believe that even the 50 percent genetically endowed set point can be boosted through a variety of means. These include exercise, behavioral cognitive therapy, and even something as simple as expressing gratitude each and every day.

As Meister Eckhart eloquently said, "If the only prayer you say in your life is thank you, that would suffice."

Traditionally, it has been thought that people generally return to a baseline level of happiness after joyous or sad events. This phenomenon has been referred to as *hedonic adaptation*. Evidence shows that even mega lottery winners return to their set point baseline a year later. Indeed, some are less happy. The only lottery winners who are happier are those who donate some of their windfall to charity and who use their newfound wealth to have meaningful experiences.

Happiness, as we can see, is a choice.

Choose wisely.

Joy is found by savoring your experiences, what the poet John Keats called "moments big as years."

LIVING ONLINE OR IN THE MOMENT

In great part, choosing happiness equates to the decision to forge strong connections with other people. As the world becomes increasingly digital, intrapersonal communication through social media and texting can come to take the place of face-to-face conversations and of interpersonal connections. The observation here is simple: choose happiness by putting down the phone, coming out from behind the screen, and connecting face-to-face.

If we rely on electronics as the conduit of a relationship, we create a false sense of relationships, and in this void of human connection comes anxiety and depression. A recent study of three hundred university students demonstrated this correlation.[3] The amount of time that the students spent on their phones was negatively correlated with their mental health. In other words, the more time spent with electronics, the less content they felt. The correlation between mental health and the reliance on electronics goes even deeper than the measurement of time spent with the devices. It comes down to intention. For those individuals who indicated that they were simply alleviating boredom with their electronic toys, there was not a significant relationship between the electronics and poor mental health, but when the intention was to use electronics to cope with or escape from anxiety-producing situations, the study participants showed troubling scores on the mental health questionnaire. Escaping day-to-day life through electronics can negatively impact mental health and exacerbate unhealthy predispositions.

The study showed that the type of online activity being used matters, too, and here is where research indicates that social media can be dangerous. One study showed that time spent on Facebook can lead to feelings of envy and depression.[4] Comparing ourselves to others fuels negative psychology and makes us less willing to reach out generously to others. When we feel envy, anxiety, and depression, we shut down.

PURPOSE, LONGEVITY, AND HEALTH

While being happy and living with purpose are correlated, the work of a Florida State University research lab guides us in understanding the distinction between a happy life and a meaningful life.[5] Here are some of the variables:

- ◆ Our relationship to time matters. Meaningfulness arises from thoughtful consideration of the past, present, and future, but happy people tend to focus on the present. Happiness is of the moment, in the moment, whereas meaningfulness persists across time.
- ◆ Happiness arises from giving to others. This finding confirms the adage that it is better to give than to receive.
- ◆ Pushing ourselves is important to feeling happy and purposeful. Meaningful lives are not stress-free. They involve challenges and problem-solving. Engaging in challenges nudges us out of our comfort zone and gives a new perspective that helps us to find meaning. We arrive at new insights about our purpose after we have experienced a great challenge; struggling helps us understand, from a new or bigger perspective, how the pieces of our lives fit together, and how we relate to others.

Having a purpose in life reduces stress, which, in turn, reduces substance abuse, anxiety, and depression. A sense of meaningfulness can even help manage pain. A 2006 University of Missouri study, published in *Integrative Medicine Insights*, found that believing in God helped African American women to address the pain and the anxiety of a diagnosis of breast cancer.[6] Researchers found that this spiritual sense of purpose also led to patients wanting to be more informed, prodding them to seek information about their health condition.

Having a purpose in life reduces stress, which, in turn, reduces substance abuse, anxiety, and depression. A sense of meaningfulness can even help manage pain.

Richard J. Leider, author and CEO of the Inventure Group, says purpose in life can be found through self-exploration. Reflection, meditation, journaling, and prayer are suggested methods of maintaining a positive outlook. When you look closely, you see that these are all methods that help you uncover your purpose in life.

Leider posits that the sense of life purpose and the length of the life span are closely related. He says, "Death gives instruction to life; the longer we live, the more we grow to understand that compassion is the main lesson that we are here to learn. Compassion is the inner urge we feel to give our gifts to others. . . . The ultimate purpose in life is to die happy; the way to die happy is to be thoroughly used up before we pass on—to be used for the sake of a purpose considered by ourselves as a worthy one."[7]

Living with a sense of purpose has been strongly linked to health and longevity, with anecdotal illustrations of death directly linked to loss of purpose. In other words, not having a life purpose increases disease risk and shortens life span. The absence of a reason to get out of bed in the morning translates into dying prematurely. One longitudinal study examined stroke victims and correlated their psychological health data with postmortem causes of stroke. Those with no sense of purpose were 46 percent more likely to have died of a stroke.

Most studies on the benefits of compassion and thankfulness rely on self-reporting—that is, subjects are asked to describe how they feel before and after the study activities, and researchers, more or less, take their word for it. In 2015, Paul Mills and colleagues took traditional gratitude research to a more quantifiable level.[8] They studied 186 men and women with asymptomatic heart failure and its association with gratitude, spiritual well-being, sleep, mood, fatigue, and inflammation. For an eight-week period some of the patients were asked to write down three things for which they were grateful.

The researchers found a correlation between the magnitude of gratitude expression and circulating levels of several important inflammatory biomarkers. An exciting finding was that gratitude and spiritual well-being related to improved mood and sleep. As Paul Mills so eloquently summed it up, "It seems that a more grateful heart is indeed a more healthy heart, and that gratitude journaling is an easy way to support cardiac health."[9]

From these studies and others comes actionable advice:

Reach out to others to avoid loneliness and thereby increase your sense of purpose.

Find your life's purpose and you will take better care of your health. You will be healthier, and your life span will be longer.

Also, living a service-oriented life keeps you feeling needed and surrounded by the people and things you love.

Reading this may stir a yearning in you to find your purpose. A cautionary tale here—many find their purpose through work, but it can sometimes lead to excess and, eventually, a decrease in health.

THE STRESS OF OVERWORK CAN KILL YOU

Karōshi is a Japanese word that means death caused by job-related exhaustion. *Karōshi*-related deaths are on the rise in Japan, where the government has officially begun maintaining statistics and compensating families. Lack of strong labor laws in Japan is resulting in a higher incidence of long hours spent compulsively working to the point of exhaustion. Particularly among young or female Japanese workers, there is a high degree of strain resulting from the demand for labor.

Rather than hiring more workers, employers are squeezing more out of their current employees. Work-related suicides, known as *karōjisatsu*, have increased 45 percent in the past four years for those twenty-nine and younger, and this rate was up 39 percent among women in general. This is due in large part to a two-tier working system, with regular employees receiving benefits and improved working conditions, whereas temporarily contracted, nonregular employees are suffering fatalities caused by overwork.

Sadly, this condition is being recognized as a worldwide phenomenon and has been documented in several countries, including China, England, Indonesia, and France.

Researchers at the Harvard T. H. Chan School of Public Health have found that optimism is linked to healthier hearts. Among those with an established risk for heart problems, those with happier outlooks were less likely to have strokes or heart attacks. Having a better sense of well-being leads to healthier lifestyles and better sleeping habits. While many studies have focused on the correlation between depression and mortality and the negative effects anxiety has on heart health, these recent studies have shifted gears to focus on how optimism aids health and produces a longer life span.

It has been well documented that fear, hate, anger, anxiety, and stress all cause damage to the body, but what about the effects of love, joy, and hope? Is there a measurable benefit of positivity? The discussion is generally framed in terms of presence of stressors versus the absence of stressors, but recent studies have shifted the balance to look at the benefit of having a positive outlook.

HAPPY IS AS HAPPY DOES

Perhaps Winston Churchill said it best: "A pessimist sees the difficulty in every opportunity. An optimist sees the opportunity in every difficulty."

Studies show that stress in early childhood can result in a physiological response that leads a multitude of adverse effects on the body and the nervous system. This stress can linger long into adulthood, yet this stress response can be unlearned through behavioral therapy and a conscious practice of focusing on the positive.

The pathway to well-being can be found in these four components:

- Emotional vitality that is evident through enthusiasm, hopefulness, and engagement
- Optimism about future events
- A supportive network of family and friends
- Strong ability to self-regulate and understand oneself

Professor Laura Kubzansky of the Harvard T. H. Chan School of Public Health has found that optimism alone cuts coronary disease risk in half. She and a handful of others have been at the vanguard of suggesting the beneficial effect of exhibiting a positive outlook on life. Her goal is to ensure broad understanding that cultivating a positive outlook is on par with other such health initiatives as good eating, exercise, and all things in moderation.

A landmark seventy-five-year longitudinal study, known as the Harvard Grant Study, answers the question "How can you live long and be happy?"[10] At its core, the study finds that longevity and happiness are predicated by good relationships. The seminal message is that good relationships keep us happier and healthier. Trusted relationships even protect our brains from cognitive decline.

Social connectedness and the quality of our relationships with both family and friends are good for us, whereas loneliness is toxic. The study found that it's not the number of friends you have at age fifty but the quality of your relationships that matter. In fact, your satisfaction with relationships at age fifty is more important than your cholesterol levels as a determinant of health and happiness three decades later at age eighty! You can hear all about this exciting longitudinal study from its director, psychiatrist Robert Waldinger, in his compelling TED Talk.[11]

As Mark Twain put it, "There isn't time—so brief is life— for bickerings, apologies, heartburnings, callings to account. There is only time for loving—and but an instant, so to speak, for that."

THE POWER OF A SMILE

We've established that modern behavioral science has helped answer one of humanity's oldest questions: What is the nature of human happiness? The academic field of psychology has developed a new branch focused on how to cultivate joy. This science of happiness has emerged in the last twenty years as behavioral scientists put their own stake in the ground to join in the debate of this essential yet ephemeral state called happiness—many consider it the very point of existence—the ultimate goal and the quintessential accomplishment.

Previously, the role of happiness in human life was the exclusive purview of poets and philosophers. It was once thought happiness was bestowed on a select few—kings, nobility, and wealthy merchants. Socrates argued otherwise and claimed that happiness could be achieved by human endeavor. The ancient Greeks coined a word to describe this state of mind—*eudaimonia*, which literally translates into *human flourishing*.

As Mark Twain put it, "There isn't time—so brief is life— for bickerings, apologies, heartburnings, callings to account. There is only time for loving—and but an instant, so to speak, for that."

Now researchers across many disciplines have begun earnest study of the subject, each holding their own view of the antecedents, feelings, and consequences of being happy. Happiness can be defined and studied in many ways. Psychologists study what people feel, economists study what people value, and neuroscientists study how the brain physically responds to rewards. These are three different perspectives of what it means to be happy, and progress in any of these fields supports the advancements of the others. The work is all interrelated.

Scientific inquiry traditionally has cautiously addressed subjective experiences like emotion, as it is difficult to quantify something as ephemeral as happiness. However, with proper experimental design, consensus is easier to reach than previously imagined. There are several working designs used to study happiness, but the simplest is posing the question: *How do you feel right now?* Subjects and researchers alike can trust that the question is understood and can be accurately answered. There is a whole area of science called *psychometrics* that focuses on the accuracy of measurement, and it turns out that numerous surveys and other measurement tools have been shown to be psychometrically sound.[12]

Answers can be given on a scale of 1 to 10. Any differences between subjective quantification (e.g., one person's rating of 4 is another one's 7) will be accounted for with a large population. Another method for data gathering is to use magnetic resonance imaging (MRI) to measure cerebral blood flow, watching where the elixir flows when the question is asked. Likewise, electromyography can measure the activity of muscles responsible for smiling, an action prompted by feelings of well-being and happiness. Each of these methods yields data that support the following themes.[13]

First, the makeup of happiness is fairly predictable. Typically, people in romantic relationships are happier than those who are not, healthy people are happier than those who are sick, rich are happier than those who are poor, and churchgoers are happier than those who do not attend church.[14] However, these things almost never lead to more sustained happiness. In fact, it seems that people are not good at predicting what will make them happy, and their desires change from day to day. This is good, because most experiences with happiness, for good or bad, affect us for about three months, at which point we return to our happiness set point.

Second, people are more resilient than they think and almost always come through bad experiences or tragedies feeling stronger. In part, this is the result of not knowing what will make you happy, and it is also related to a third finding that is ubiquitous in studies of happiness: people are very good at finding silver linings. This is known as *synthesizing happiness*, which is what we produce when we don't get exactly what we want. Natural happiness is what we feel when we *do* get what we want. While synthetic happiness is not quite the same as the real thing, it is still good. Any happiness, synthetic or natural, has great impact on our lives and our chemistry.

It is interesting to think about whether happiness has a function. Happiness is certainly central to guiding most people's attention; we gravitate toward what makes us happy, and we move away from what makes us sad or angry. Scientists have asked a few interesting questions regarding the importance of this in a variety of life settings.

DOES HAPPINESS AFFECT CREATIVITY?

The image of the passionate and morose artist has been stamped onto our cultural conditioning, but does misery equate to muse? Must artists struggle? Not so, according to the research. Various studies show that miserable people are not the most creative. The Van Goghs and Beethovens are the exception, not the rule. It is, in fact, the happy ones who are more creative, especially because they are also more productive, which sets up a positive feedback loop. Their happiness encourages the work that encourages the happiness and so on and so on. How fortunate we would all be to live in that cycle. That is the secret to never "working" a single day in one's life.

It should come as no surprise that productivity leads to happiness. In studies of employee happiness, it was discovered that people like to be challenged and like to be productive. Challenges must be appropriate to skill, as most folks wither when they feel threatened or overwhelmed. Neuroscientists studying physiological happiness have consistently found that reward always works better than threats in motivating employees with a satisfying challenge.[15]

In the end, all scientific data point to the social element of happiness. We are happy within a network of others. It is so systematic that how a person feels can be easily read by studying that person's social network—friends, family, partners, and all the bonds made with those nearby. A key component in the scientific study of happiness is this social mandate.

FAKE IT UNTIL YOU MAKE IT

Every culture experiences happiness, and every culture uses smiles to transmit happiness to others. A genuine smile—truly a universal expression—allows the subjective quality of happiness to be considered objective in that it is verifiable by others. The urge to smile when happy is, in a sense, hardwired into us. We do not learn the behavior by observing others, as evidenced by the fact that individuals who were born blind also flash a brilliant smile when they are happy.

Not only can science objectively study happiness, it can even find ways to bring happiness to you. The simple phrase "Fake it till you make it" finds application in this area through the phenomenon of smiling. It has been proven that the act of smiling will elevate your mood, bringing happiness where there was none. Facial feedback response theory holds that when you activate smiling muscles, you quickly release the neurotransmitters responsible for the emotion of joy. In broader terms, this theory states that simulation of an emotion can cause that emotion. People smile when they are happy, and it turns out that people are also happy when they smile. And everyone knows how to smile.

Andrew Newberg claimed that smiling is the "symbol rated with the highest possible emotional content." A Papua New Guinea tribe with no exposure to Western civilization uses smiles to communicate happiness and understood a smile when they saw one. Prebirth studies indicated that babies smile in the womb and just keep on doing so when they are born. In fact, children smile about four hundred times a day, whereas a happy adult typically only manages forty to fifty grins. Some adults only get in twenty or so a day, making children about twenty times as happy. This is in keeping with most frequently recorded behavioral observations in children.[16]

It may be no surprise that smiles are contagious, but why?[17] Mimicking smiles is a vital part of understanding the connection between smiling and happiness and the social bonds these facial expressions forge. Our ability to mimic a smile greatly influences our ability to determine if others' smiles are genuine. Without the ability to reproduce it ourselves, it is difficult to connect through smiling. In addition, whether a smile is genuine or not can influence how we react to the person who is smiling and whether it influences our own happiness level.

When a real smile graces a face, we know it. Scientists have been examining just how we can tell real from fake, and it may surprise you to know that the answer is quite physiological. Different muscle groups are used in fake smiling versus genuine smiling. Social smiles use the zygomaticus major, muscles that control the corners of the mouth and are responsible for the upward curve of a smile.[18]

In a real smile, the extraocular muscles around the eye sockets engage. That's why we look into others' eyes to see how they really feel, even if they are smiling. Our brains compare the geometry in a person's face to a genuine smile from previous experience. It is like comparing this smile to the average template of smiling that we mentally have abstracted across the years from all kinds of social interactions. Our minds evaluate whether the situation calls for a smile, and we subconsciously mimic the person's smile, testing it out. Does it match? Does it reflect and generate a feeling of happiness?

When the smile is real, what is going on in the brain? Neuronal signals travel from the cortex to the brain stem and on down into the smiling muscles in the face. When these muscles engage, they send feedback to the brain, saying, "Hey, we're happy!" This creates a cycle of happiness, "stimulating the brain's reward systems in a way that even chocolate, a well-regarded pleasure inducer, cannot match."

The act of smiling is proven to affect levels of cortisol, dopamine, adrenaline, and endorphins—all biochemical factors in happiness. This chemical cascade creates a positive feedback loop of happiness as endorphins are produced and neuronal signals are transmitted to facial muscles that then send a signal back to the brain, producing more endorphins.

MIRROR, MIRROR

But there is even more to it than pleasant chemicals. It turns out that there are specialized cells in the brain whose function it is to share the emotions and actions of others.

Have you ever used the phrase "I feel you"? It does seem that we feel each other's pains and joys, and researchers may have discovered exactly where that sense comes from. Certain cells in the brain called *mirror neurons* have this amazing ability to mirror what another is doing.

In the 1980s, an Italian research team headed by Giacomo Rizzolatti at the University of Parma in Italy studied brain activity in macaques.[19] His team had discovered that certain brain cells lit up when the macaques reached for a peanut or other food treat. Some cells fired at the sight of a peanut, and others had to have the researcher grasp the peanut and pick it up before they fired.

To their surprise, the cells fired not only when the macaque reached for the peanut but also when the *researcher* reached for the peanut! Thanks to a serendipitous moment, Rizzolatti happened to have probes in the right area of the brain at the right time to discover mirror neurons. The Rizzolatti experimental team started getting more systematic.

There seemed to be rules at play where vision was not enough and grasping was not enough; it was as if these cells were waiting for another macaque or human to grasp the peanut with his or her fingers in the same way as the test macaque. In a routine exploration, they decided to study how the cells reacted to objects other than peanuts.

Mirror neurons are brain cells that fire equally when we perform an action or when we watch someone else perform the same action. Located in the premotor cortex, an area responsible for action and planning movement, it is believed that they are closely linked to empathy. This is understandable, considering they are instrumental in mimicry and allow primates to learn vicariously through watching others.

It is still unclear how human brains use this mirror neuron system or if we even have the same sort of specific mirror cells as our macaque cousins. Researchers are not routinely allowed to attach electrodes directly to human brains. That hasn't stopped scientists from exploring the monumental implications mirror neurons present for the study of social behavior.

These cells may play a role in autism and language development. They certainly produce empathy and likely are important for developing an understanding of emotional states and reactions to environmental stimuli.

Mirror neurons are why smiling at a baby causes the baby to mirror back the smile. They are the reason we flinch when we watch skateboarders wipe out on the library stairs. They are likely the basis for an interesting treatment for phantom pain, which is a condition that sometimes arises after an arm or leg has been amputated. The person experiences pain, itching, or other intense sensations in the missing body part.

How can you scratch an itch on your leg when it is not there? The itching or pain can get maddening, but medical experts have shown that the sensations are real. They arise in the spinal cord and are not just in the imagination. But how do you treat phantom sensations? Thanks to mirror neurons, the solution is easy, noninvasive, and free. If you seat the patient across from another individual who scratches his or her own leg in just the right spot, suddenly the phantom itch in the patient's amputated leg goes away.

At the very least, it seems that we are fundamentally hardwired to understand each other's pains and pleasures. As social creatures, humans and monkeys share the need for empathy, communication, and caring. It would make sense that we share a neurological system allowing for such behaviors. This mirror neuron system points to how hardwired happiness and social behavior are.

Happiness and smiling are desirable, even beneficial, to life and humanity. Mother Teresa said, "We shall never know all the good that a simple smile can do." Scientists have already quantified many of the effects of smiling on happiness, even beyond neurochemicals and feedback loops.

One study discovered that the brain keeps track of all smiles, and all smiles affect the brain. Smiles reduce stress levels, which means that they reduce the amount of cortisol circulating throughout the bloodstream and generate positive emotions that have significant impact on health and psyche. The feedback loop combined with the contagious nature of smiling makes a smiling individual very attractive to others. When you smile, other people smile, too, and thereby begins the loop that will send them on a happiness-filled jaunt. This is a real cause for joy because a happier person lives a longer and healthier life.

In a retrospective longitudinal study, baseball cards were scrutinized to determine the importance of smiling to health. Pre-1950s baseball cards were studied for their smiles. Those players who did not smile in their photos were found to live approximately 72.9 years, while those who did smile lived up to 79.9 years.[20] If smiling indicates happiness and also longevity, then perhaps happiness indicates health. In another study, yearbook pictures were used to accurately predict happiness in life. Those individuals whose photos exhibited genuine smiles stayed happy throughout life. Interesting follow-up research could also explore how long these people live.

So if smiling is the key to happiness, and happiness is the meaning of life, what can we do to amplify our smile power? Practice makes perfect, and that goes for happiness as well. Perfecting smiling can lead to a better quality of life and will always be happy work.

SMILE BOOSTERS

Here is some advice for better smiling. Think of a happy event or a loved one or a memory of a time you displayed a genuine smile. Re-create it in front of a mirror, and take note of which muscles are being used. Discover your own face and become comfortable with it. Smiling is a joy to yourself and others, so do not be ashamed or embarrassed. It has been noted that women smile more easily than men and can more easily detect the difference between a fake smile and genuine smile. The social predilections of women and their penchant for reading the needs and motivations of others may be the driver behind this innate skill. At any rate, trying on a genuine smile before entering a stressful event can mean the difference between happiness and angry disappointment.

When it comes to smiles and happiness, it turns out that frequency is greater than intensity. Many small, positive occurrences produce more happiness than one big, positive event. Each day, it is important to wear good shoes, kiss someone, or sneak a french fry—you don't have to win the lottery. Equate building happiness to building muscles. You don't need a big event or a magic pill. You need small, consistent actions that add up over time.

These daily wins amount to a lifetime of happiness when you look back at the end of the day. Meditating, exercising, and getting good sleep all count toward these little bits of happiness. Among these acts is helping others. Helping others will give you a boost, as will nurturing social connections. It is important to remember that happiness is a social emotion. And always be mindful of your feelings—write down what you are grateful for, how you feel, and why you feel it. Like weight loss, the secret of happiness is no secret, but rather it is conventional wisdom.

That's not to say there is nothing left to learn about happiness. Future research can answer many remaining questions. When are people happy? Do we want lives free of heartache, or is there value in negative experiences? This strikes at another important focus for research: separation of happiness and life satisfaction. People with children are reportedly less happy on a moment-to-moment basis but have a lifetime fulfillment that those without children do not have. This is the difference between daily happiness and the summation of all happy moments. These are separate categories entirely that research needs to hone and further define. Happiness, we believe, is more than the sum of happy moments.

Research has revealed a great deal about the cause, process, and effect of happiness. How we use that information remains to be seen in our day-to-day actions. Science can tell us how to live the life we want, but nothing can tell us how to choose the life we want. That will always be up to us to decide.

STRIKE A POSE: YOGA BUILDS RESILIENCE AND HAPPINESS

What we decide to do with our precious time—ranging from momentarily flashing a smile to indulging in a cozy afternoon reading to pursuing a career that we find fulfilling—has a tremendous impact on our happiness, health, and longevity. Here we discuss some activities to consider as a direct route to finding contentment, joy, and peace.

In the United States, there has been a significant increase in the number of individuals who practice yoga. This ancient practice evolved in India over centuries but is now seeing its heyday in the modern world. And it's getting more popular year by year. Yoga is best known in the West for its stretchy, sometimes difficult and contorted poses. And, to be fair, there is some of that. But stretching is not the point.

The term *yoga* is a Sanskrit word that means "to yoke together." What is it we are yoking or joining together? It's this: mind, body, and spirit. The power of yoga comes intentionally from using this well-crafted method of moving the body, breathing with awareness, and focusing attention to train the brain and body, ushering us toward a peaceful mind and better health.

If you've resisted trying yoga in the past, let us invite you to reconsider. One of the most popular excuses that people give for not trying yoga is that they aren't sufficiently flexible. We politely suggest that this is an oxymoron. To say that you are not flexible enough to do yoga is like saying you are too dirty to take a bath.

In the last ten years or so, there has been a massive surge in the amount of attention researchers have given to exploring the benefits of practicing yoga. In a true melding of mind and spirit, some scientists have even been inspired to switch to yoga research as a career after they turned on to yoga themselves for rehabilitation or to alleviate a physical ailment. Many found that the practice gave them an elusive sense of calm that had been missing from their lives, something that is difficult to achieve in a high-pressure, publish-or-perish academic environment.[21]

Yoga is not an easy topic to study—anything that has multiple interacting components, like movement, breath, physiology, and mood, is challenging to put under the microscope. While it may not be easy to quantify the results of a yoga practice, it is not impossible. In fact, some giant steps have been made in understanding how yoga is measured and the theory around why it works.

There are now hundreds of published research studies about the health and wellness benefits of yoga for individuals with cancer, anxiety, depression, arthritis, heart disease, musculoskeletal disorders, chronic pain, and many other conditions. These scientific studies support that yoga improves mental health and builds psychological resistance.[22] Yoga researchers are starting to crack the code on what the chemistry is in the nervous system that supports these mental changes.[23]

Timothy McCall is a physician who has become a worldwide voice advocating for yoga as medicine. He teaches all over the world on how to develop a yoga practice that best suits an individual's body and a variety of medical conditions. He is part of a new wave of health care professionals called yoga therapists who are starting to bridge Eastern contemplative practices with the Western medical system. There are many general patterns that fall out of the work of McCall and his yoga therapy cohorts. As you will see below, these effects can impact many disease states for the better, supporting the premise that practicing yoga can alleviate suffering in different ways.

Yoga has been shown to offer these benefits:

- Increasing muscle strength
- Improving posture and protecting the spine

- Increasing blood flow and lymph flow
- Boosting immunity
- Decreasing cortisol levels
- Lowering blood sugar
- Improving sleep
- Balancing the digestive system
- Reducing pain
- It may even lower your golf handicap[24]

This is just a starter list of the benefits. Hopefully, it is more than enough to encourage you to reach for a yoga mat.

The good news is that you do not have to be a body-contorting monk living in a cave high up in the Himalayas to reap these benefits for yourself. In fact, the recommendations of senior yoga practitioners converge quite nicely with the scientific evidence. Both show that immediate benefits of yoga can be achieved in just seven minutes of mindful stretching. There are even apps that can guide a seven-minute practice.[25] Seven minutes! We can all fit seven minutes into our day to bring greater calm and joy in the rest of our days. There are examples of yoga postures, flows, and instructions online that can guide you in how seven magic minutes lead you to happiness.[26]

There is no one magic yoga posture that unlocks the key to happiness. While it is not easy to draw a line between a specific posture and the psychological benefits, it is firmly rooted in evidence that there is a correlation between having a regular yoga practice and feeling less mood disruption and more happiness. We know that there is a connection, just like we know that jutting your chest forward will make you feel more confident and crossing your arms will make you feel less confident.

Some anecdotal wisdom shows us that some yoga postures are better for calming and relaxing the nervous system while others are better for boosting energy, vigor, and confidence.[27] We're confident that yoga researchers will continue to understand how different postures alter the biochemical pathways that support all these biopsychosocial benefits.

DON'T JUST DO SOMETHING— SIT THERE!

Meditation is a practice of training your mind to focus on a single point. Some people think of it as the discipline of clearing your mind of all thoughts, but it is so much more.

Meditation involves placing a laser-like focus on the self and doing it effortlessly. Like sharpening the blade of a knife, meditation sharpens our cognitive and emotional abilities to cut through to the true self. It reduces the noise and leaves behind a clear life signal. The noise left behind is distraction, irritation, and negative emotion. With meditation, we aren't as cluttered or burdened, and we are able to show up as our best selves, full of purpose, enthusiasm, and compassion. If life feels out of control, meditation is the way to get it under control.

Recent studies have shown that meditation, like yoga, has numerous basic physiological benefits:

- Lowers blood pressure
- Slows breathing rate

- Improves rest and sleep
- Boosts immunity
- Lessens stress
- Increases telomere length[28]

Just to explain that last bullet a bit, let's pause and consider the implications of lengthening our telomeres. Telomeres are little endcaps on our chromosomes that serve a protective function so that when cells throughout our bodies replicate, they continue to do so free of error. The telomere endcaps keep the gene-copying process happening accurately. Moreover, how robust and long these telomeres are correlates with the length of one's life span.

Telomere length is correlated with longevity: the longer the telomeres, the longer the life span. This research earned Elizabeth Blackburn the Nobel Prize in Physiology or Medicine in 2009.

Solid research shows that people who are chronically stressed—let's take mothers of disabled children as an example—have shortened telomeres. Telomeres are longer in individuals who regularly exercise, but lengthening your telomeres doesn't have to be laborious once you wake up and smell the coffee.

Telomeres are also longer in individuals who meditate. In many ways, meditation is similar to yoga. It has tremendous benefits that accrue over time. In other words, longtime meditators have different brains from those of everyone else. This was assumed to be the case for decades, well before we had a snapshot that proved that it is definitively true, as verified by fMRI images. Harvard researcher Sara Lazar published a groundbreaking study that showed what was happening in the brains of longtime meditators. To be more specific, she showed what was *not* happening in these brains as compared to the brains of non-meditators.

Lazar and her colleagues were the first to show that the practice of meditation produces measurable differences in the brain.[29] What was compelling, however, is that these differences revealed themselves with only two weeks of practice. Study participants were divided into two groups. The experimental group was taught how to meditate. They were introduced to guided mindfulness meditation focusing on how to increase nonjudgmental/nonreactive awareness of sensations, emotions, and state of mind. The control group did not learn meditation. Before and after the eight-week study, both groups completed a series of self-reported psychological questionnaires and underwent brain scans.

The results were remarkable. The meditators showed significant improvement across eight weeks in their questionnaire scores, but even more compellingly, they showed enhanced brain activity in regions that are known to be involved in attention, memory, and emotion. Importantly, there were structural changes in the amygdala, a pair of tiny almond-shaped structures in the brain that process fear and anger. The reduction in amygdala activity correlated with experiencing less negative emotion.

So, yes, there really is something about mindfulness. No, it is not just a fad. It actually changes your brain. It transforms you into a better version of yourself. Mindfulness and meditation really do make us happier.[30]

The story of Shannon Paige is quite telling. A yoga teacher, entrepreneur, and activist, Paige found out that surviving cancer treatment does not equal healing. When she was twenty-one years old, she was devastated to receive a cancer diagnosis. She put up a vigorous and brave fight. This meant rounds of chemo and a hysterectomy. She kept going. She survived. Then she began to feel guilty when people celebrated her healing. These were well-intentioned friends and family members who were thrilled she had survived her cancer—except she did not feel whole. She felt paralyzed by depression, only barely able to muster a smile for the other person's benefit.[31]

Her Boulder physician gave her a radical prescription—she had to start yoga. Thus began a journey of understanding the healing potential of mindfulness. In a way, *mindfulness is also bodyfulness*, and it was exactly what Paige needed after her body had been ravaged by cancer and then decimated again by the cure. She needed to be integrated back into her body.

Paying attention to the breath shifts the habitual patterns of the brain. These are the gifts of a mindfulness practice like meditation or yoga: feeling alive, more visceral, greatly aware of sensation, and skillful at starting to dissect the spaces between stimulus and response. And it is here where healing happens and wholeness is restored. She came full circle. Paige is now a renowned expert on how restorative yoga heals depression and anxiety. She is restored.

Mindfulness also has been found to radiate benefits beyond the individual who is practicing it. Personal mindfulness makes you more receptive to your interactions with your peers and has tremendous influence on parenting. It has been found that teaching your children to be mindful is a terrific way to help them deal with emotional and hormonal struggles. However, even if you don't actively instruct the children on how to practice mindfulness, they will still benefit from your own sense of calm and connection. We've all heard it said that if Mom is happy, everyone is happy, and there is a kernel of truth to that age-old cliché.

The Greater Good Science Center in Berkeley, California, reviewed multiple studies on the benefits of mindful parenting.[32] In a study at the University of Vermont, researchers found that parents engaging in mindfulness practice demonstrated more positive parenting practices as well. This was, in turn, associated with lower levels of stress and anxiety in their kids. While the correlation was based on parental self-report, which means the parents reported their children's reduced anxiety, the study paved the way for further studies of the benefits of mindfulness.

Indeed, in a novel study, another team of scientists demonstrated the cascading beneficial effects of mindfulness. Not only did the individuals practicing mindfulness report well-being, but, through use of functional MRI, it was found that the parents who had the greatest activation of the left anterior insular and inferior frontal gyrus had children who reported the greatest improvement in the relationship with the mindful parent.[33]

The neuroscience of mindfulness is the next frontier. It is where we are going, building upon the basics of what we know about the neurochemistry of mood and cognition.

THE NEUROCHEMISTRY
OF HAPPINESS

Happiness is central to human existence. Whether it is the central driver of all behavior or simply a chemical side effect that makes patches of biological life pleasant, the emotion of joy is found every day, in thousands of manifestations, in billions of people. The positive experience of life keeps us going. Happiness and a positive outlook are strongly interconnected, and it is possible to generate one through stimulation of the other. It is well known that being happy powers our optimism, but have you tried to use optimism to create feelings of bliss?

Experience shapes how our brains and nervous systems are designed. When an experience is undertaken, new lines connect the neural dots, forming a biological road map of the experience. Later neurological impulses follow this map more easily than blazing their own trail, so familiar experiences and reactions become, in effect, easier to have. Basically, the more frequently you experience happiness in its various forms, the easier it is to be happy. In an interview with the host of the podcast *The Greater Good*, Michael Bergeisen, neuroscientist and mindfulness expert Rick Hanson outlines how to focus mental energy to change your brain for the better.

Hanson asserts that daily practices can increase the "mapping" of your brain's happy pathways. He suggests that you should practice being aware of body sensations, like breathing, to thicken insula in the brain, allowing neurons to connect strongly to one another.[34] In addition, focusing on your own body and emotions leads to better understanding of yourself and others. This results in lower stress levels, especially in tense meetings. On the other hand, negative thoughts impede the building of strong happiness connections in the brain.

It is less risky to assume the worst and be wrong than it is to assume the best and be wrong. This is called negativity bias, and it is evolutionarily hardwired into our brains. Once something bad happens, we do not see it as just one negative event. When we dwell on that event, we add meaning where there is none, and we subsequently strengthen those bad-experience pathways. This makes us overrepresent the importance of the event.

The fix? When that first event happens, surround yourself with positive thoughts to keep that same dart from hitting you over and over. Try not to see threats where there are none. Negativity can protect us from danger, but it also creates enemies where there are none. Don't give bad thoughts an express lane through your brain.

This optimistic padding is vital to happiness. The brain attaches wide, generalized importance to specific events. This is known as *implicit memory* and can lead to all sorts of bias and bias confirmation. When a loved one offends us, there is a strong likelihood that we will generalize the specific negative feeling arising from that specific event to every other aspect of our feelings. Hurt feelings over a missed birthday can be remembered as a general feeling of neglect in all areas. It was found that negative interactions are five times as powerful as positive interactions in a relationship. To cope with this, make sure to think five times as many good thoughts about your partner as negative thoughts. And remember that spats and quarrels will present disproportionately larger in your memory, so cut your partner some slack and you will make yourself happier.

Dwelling on the positive is a great way to fight the power of negative thoughts. Applying your mental faculties in this way can accomplish a good deal. In addition to the power of focus and self-examination, good old-fashioned education can help lubricate the everyday grind. Studying how the brain influences emotions allows you to differentiate when something calls for tears and when it is being overblown as a primitive defense mechanism. Emotional intelligence is a skill that can be refined and learned, just like calculus or martial arts or learning to play the guitar.

In other words, when we distill the ingredients in the recipe to cook up happiness, we find that the essential ingredient, the saffron of happiness, is our pattern of thoughts. Our subjective view of an event matters more than the event itself.

To further extrapolate, one can be socially engaged to create positive change. This means that you can offer your thoughts and emotions as a conduit to generate more goodness in the world, dedicating yourself and your skills to worthy causes. This transference of thought with intent to do good in the world is at the heart of having a life purpose.

Learning is good medicine. When we learn new information and skills, we engage a process of systematically rewiring our brains. We literally change the structure of the brain through building new connections, causing cells to link together to talk to each other in different and more sophisticated ways. The technical term for this process by which the brain changes itself is *neuroplasticity*. It points to how the architecture of the brain is malleable, like plastic—the structure is not set in stone.

Neuroplasticity means that the brain can rewire itself. This is such uplifting news. It means we can slide right into the driver's seat and steer ourselves on the grand course of the nature-versus-nurture debate. Changing thought patterns and habits means that the brain is constantly reorganizing and rebuilding itself.

Popular media tends to talk about neuroplasticity as if it is cutting-edge research. Not to downplay the importance of this discovery, because it was certainly revolutionary when it happened, but the foundational knowledge of neuroplasticity is something that we've known about for more than a generation. It is true that the pioneering neuroscientists of the 1800s and early 1900s thought that after a certain point of infant development, the architecture of the human brain became static. While this view lingered until the 1960s, by then some neuroscientists were beginning to see strong evidence that challenged that fundamental tenet of their discipline. In short, they saw that *neurons that fire together wire together.*

Today, it is well established that neural pathways evolve throughout the entire life span. Modern neuroscientists are now tracking down how the signaling chemicals of neuroplasticity, such as nerve growth factor and the brain-derived neurotrophic factor, can put a smart structural cascade of physical changes in place that allow us to learn and become more mentally and emotionally adept throughout our lifetime.

Neuroplasticity is at the heart of behavioral and emotional resilience. In short, we become stronger by being lifelong learners. How we think, what we do, what we observe, the friends we make—these things alter the very structure of the brain. In other words, it pays for the old dog to keep learning new tricks.

For instance, the risk of dementia can be reduced by exercising more, drinking coffee, and learning new skills. Try speaking a foreign language, mastering salsa dancing, or increasing your chops in the kitchen like a master chef. The important distinction is this: learning is not about doing more crossword puzzles; it is not more of the same. It is continuously sampling what is novel and different so that you tap into and work out new mental muscles, rather than flexing the same old crossword muscle. Interestingly, even exploration of a regular meditation practice can change the structure of the brain. Although it might look like you're only sitting there and doing nothing, meditation is quite active in rewiring the synapses of the brain, and there is now an abundance of research literature on meditation and neuroplasticity.[35]

When studying the brain, there are three major factors that can be used to define this phenomenon. The electrical domain comprises brain waves. The architectural domain reflects physical structures within the brain, and the chemical—or neurochemical—domain addresses biochemical interactions between cells. These factors vary in how they define happiness for each person. To have a comprehensive understanding of happiness, it is important to examine all three, and a good place to begin is with the third domain: neurochemistry.

Neurochemicals, which are one-third of the brain triad, can basically be broken into seven chemicals that interact at different ratios within the brain, allowing each person to experience a personal or subjective view of happiness. Chemicals are responsible for most feelings of bliss and reward, as well as for feelings of fear and paranoia. It is, therefore, no surprise that studying happiness begins with studying the "feel-good" domain of the brain. The following chemicals are those that have been closely linked to happy thoughts.

[1] Endocannabinoids are endogenously produced cannabis, nicknamed "the bliss molecules." They are the molecules responsible for the euphoric "runner's high" experienced after prolonged exertion. Our bodies produce as many endocannabinoids as a mature cannabis plant. However, a good jog may be just as effective in the happiness department.

[2] The second chemical is dopamine. Dopamine causes all reward-driven behavior. It is released when we achieve a dream, no matter how small. Known as "the reward molecule," dopamine allows us to achieve greatness and enjoy ourselves as we do it. To get a rush of this chemical, set a minor goal and knock it out of the ballpark.

[3] Oxytocin is "the bonding molecule" and is released in response to hugging, intimacy, and cuddling. It increases the social reward feelings stemming from physical contact, which is so prevalent in our primate ancestors. Men have active levels of a similar chemical called vasopressin, which helps regulate physical touch and bonding. This bonding spirit can be magnified by shoulder slapping, sideways hugs, and handshakes. To amplify the effect of oxytocin in your body, engage in face-to-face conversations and hug a lot.

[4] Endorphins are a familiar chemical prized for their pain-fighting power. They are self-produced morphine and act in the same manner. Known as "the pain-killing molecule," endorphins are produced by heavy physical exertion, injury,

acupuncture, sexual intercourse, and orgasm. To increase the amount of endorphin-driven bliss in your life, engage in regular physical exercise, especially aerobic exercise. For best results, make that exercise sexual in nature too.

[5] The fifth chemical is GABA, "the antianxiety molecule." As might be expected, it lowers cortisol levels in your blood and inhibits neurons to create calmness. Think of it as the "slow down, you're moving too fast" transmitter. Experiments with yoga and meditation have shown increased GABA production after just one hour of practice. Taking a deep breath and clearing your mind helps stimulate GABA in your brain, as does any amount of meditation or yoga.

[6] Serotonin is another chemical that may be familiar, especially for those on antidepressants. This neurotransmitter is vital to our brains' function and not just in the happiness department. It allows concentration, memory, and confidence. Confidence leads to happiness, and boosting this chemical boosts self-confidence and vice versa. Try challenging yourself and rewarding success to create serotonin in your brain. Start with something small to get the cycle going. Think of it like gears on a bicycle: start with a small goal, gain confidence, gain serotonin, move on to a larger goal, gain confidence, gain serotonin, and so on.

[7] The last natural drug in your brain is the powerhouse of emergency responses: adrenaline. Known as "the energy molecule," adrenaline is central to most active expenditures of energy, regardless of origin. Primarily, it serves in the fight-or-flight response, driven by fear. This chemical spikes your heart rate and increases blood pressure, blasting blood and energy

throughout your system. Long-term effects can be detrimental, as the body uses a lot of resources during this over-clocked period of activity, but a little adrenaline can make the best of almost any situation. To provoke an adrenal response, take rapid breaths and flex your muscles, as though you were preparing to flee a lion.[36]

By dwelling on the positive, replacing negative thoughts with happier interpretations, and studying and understanding the power of the physical properties of your brain, happiness can be generated under your own power.

It is a profound fact that everything needed for the biological experience of happiness is present in your body and mind at all times.

And you have the keys to unlock it. We have just handed them to you.

It is a profound fact that everything needed for the biological experience of happiness is present in your body and mind at all times.

"Beannacht (Blessing)"
John O'Donohue

On the day when
the weight deadens
on your shoulders
and you stumble,
may the clay dance
to balance you.

And when your eyes
freeze behind
the grey window
and the ghost of loss
gets in to you,
may a flock of colours,
indigo, red, green,
and azure blue
come to awaken in you
a meadow of delight.

When the canvas frays
in the currach of thought
and a stain of ocean
blackens beneath you,
may there come across the waters
a path of yellow moonlight
to bring you safely home.

May the nourishment of the earth be yours,
may the clarity of light be yours,
may the fluency of the ocean be yours,
may the protection of the ancestors be yours.
And so may a slow
wind work these words
of love around you,
an invisible cloak
to mind your life.

4

Living with Purpose, Living with Love

Be a lamp, or a lifeboat, or a ladder. Help someone's soul heal. Walk out of your house like a shepherd.

—RUMI

Purpose often lurks in the most unexpected of places. For Mariah Smith, her life's purpose was patiently waiting to be discovered in the parking lot of a fast-food restaurant.

"I was at a Sonic with my mom and saw a homeless man. He was crouched down on the ground and had a little cart with him that probably had everything he owned in it. I looked in the backseat and saw that we had a blanket, so I got out and gave him the food that we had ordered and the blanket and he immediately wrapped the blanket around himself and started eating. That night changed my life forever, and it really opened my eyes."

At the time, Mariah was seventeen years old, a high school student in Virginia Beach, Virginia. This unexpected encounter with one homeless man lingered in Mariah's mind, haunting her, inspiring her. You see, Mariah had never gone to sleep hungry, yet her empathy was so profound that it changed her life and the lives of so many others.

Mariah's simple act of kindness was so easy. It made her yearn to do more. She began to wonder, what else could the homeless man in the parking lot have used? Which basic necessities could she have provided? What could she offer to others with similar needs? What more could she do?

Mariah's desire to serve others took root. "I had never really known the true meaning of hunger until I saw the way that man ate what I had given him. He was starving. After seeing that, I wanted to make sure that with every blanket I also gave a brown bag lunch. A peanut butter and jelly sandwich, bag of chips, cookies, piece of fruit, and a bottle of water that they can refill. I know that a blanket and a lunch do not seem like much, but to someone who is hungry and sleeping on the ground, it is the difference between being hungry and cold . . . or not."

Mariah knew firsthand what it meant to receive help from a stranger. She had been abandoned by her biological mother on Christmas Eve. Fate conspired to give her a second chance when she found foster parents who provided her with a safe, loving home. Perhaps that experience transformed her worldview and led to the assertion that everyone deserves to be safe and to know what it means to be cared for.

Mariah began making trip after trip to deliver useful goods to those in her hometown that were homeless. She soon formed a nonprofit organization called Blankets for the Homeless.[1] Mariah embarked on this work on her own, but today volunteers now deliver items directly to people on the street, rather than to shelters, which would be easier but would not have the same impact.

What Mariah calls "delivering with dignity" is a core part

of the mission. Volunteers offer those who are homeless sleeping bags, clothing, hats, ponchos, and backpacks. In the summer, they deliver sunscreen and bug spray. In the winter, they gift heavy coats and other warm clothing. By chatting with people, they are helping volunteers network to find others who are homeless and in need of assistance.

Since the inception of Blankets for the Homeless, Mariah and the other volunteers have hand-delivered more than eighty thousand blankets and lunches. They are active throughout several cities in Virginia, and the program's geographical reach continues to expand as more volunteers are inspired to sign on to help their homeless neighbors. Blankets for the Homeless has been featured in the media, resulting in the recruitment of additional volunteers who step up to help collect and distribute goods.

When Mariah gives television and radio interviews, she encourages others to keep what she calls a "blessing box" in their car, a repository that enables spontaneous generosity—on-the-spot help with things like a bottle of water, toiletries, and warm gloves.

Purpose and love are intimately intertwined, and a purposeful life is a life filled with love.

Purpose and love are intimately intertwined, and a purposeful life is a life filled with love.

For example, Mariah's purpose in life is to deliver little things that have great impact. What better example is there of making life better by making other lives better?

For many, this clarity—the alignment of head and heart—often emerges well into adulthood, if at all. Mariah is both an exception and exceptional in that she found her alignment at a young age.

Finding your own "why" is a life-changing and momentous event.

In addition to offering the psychological gratification of experiencing engagement and joy, living a purposeful life brings with it a constellation of additional benefits. Having a sense of purpose has been related to positive mood, hopefulness, and self-reported happiness in adolescents. Youth who are purpose-driven have a stabler sense of self earlier in life than do their counterparts who report feeling more aimless.[2]

Older adults who report living a life with purpose take better care of their physical health and are more proactive about seeking preventive health care services as they age.[3] In other words, they have identified something worth living for and, as a result, treat their health as a responsibility to that mission. Purposeful adults score higher on multiple assessments of mental health and physical well-being, and they live longer than average, so it really is a sense of purpose that ignites the spark of life in ways that are not yet fully understood.

A purposeful life makes us healthier and happier. It makes us live longer, more fulfilling lives. Who can argue with these benefits? The only questions that remain are these: How do we get some of that? How do we identify our unique purpose and start living it?

We all would choose to live a life of purpose. For some, purpose sometimes runs us over like a truck—perhaps quite literally. A sense of purpose may arise following a car crash or surviving a close call with death. It may awaken when we experience or observe a tragedy. We frequently hear about people who experience horrific events that result in trauma—in fact, the term *post-traumatic stress disorder* (PTSD) seems to be in the news every day. But the same experience can have the opposite effect. It can spur post-traumatic "growth."[4]

Finding your own "why" is a life-changing and momentous event.

People who experience post-traumatic growth emerge from the storms of their life more resilient and positive. In these instances, the trauma serves as a life lesson that enriches in the best possible way. Another term for this transformation is "benefit finding."

If we live with purpose, we tend to see a crisis as fundamental to our growth and evolution. In other words, we adapt and find the benefit in the situation. This post-traumatic growth is commonly found, for example, in cancer survivors. No one wants to receive a cancer diagnosis, but cancer survivors often emerge with an understanding that life is expanded and more precious. Their trauma is reframed in a way that is deeply meaningful—a rich and reflective interpretation of the initial trauma. They often see the world through new and brighter eyes.

These individuals are better able and more willing to live a mission-driven life, which—more often than not—involves serving others. You may be one of the many millions who enjoy TED Talks. These talks have become a cultural phenomenon in the last decade, prodding a zest for new ideas and big thinking. Did you ever notice that many TED speakers share their experience of a major life-changing event?

Generally offered early in the narrative, this experience is a core aspect of the storytelling. It suggests a hero who meets a challenge head-on and ends victorious. There is an ancient Greek saying: "A people are known by the heroes they crown." Through this transformative experience, an extraordinary opportunity may be discovered. Perhaps TED Talks are so popular because our brains are hardwired to follow a good story and cheer on the hero.

One talk offers an example of post-traumatic growth. Noted game designer Jane McGonigal is a strong advocate for the use of games as tools for positive psychology, suggesting that playing them can foster greater compassion and collaboration in society. Interestingly, this perspective took shape after Jane suffered a traumatic brain injury, a story she tells in her inspiring 2012 TED Talk, "The Game That Can Give You 10 Extra Years of Life."[5] We all long to hear stories of those who triumph over adversity, and Jane tells of developing a tool to help many people do just that.

In the Chinese language, this possibility of benefit finding is reflected optimistically in the word for crisis. The word is a combination of two Chinese characters. One character has a nuanced translation and refers to danger, uncertainty, or a critical juncture. The other character more easily translates into English as opportunity. From this vantage point, a crisis is not just the drama on the surface but also the opportunity to evolve in a positive way.

It is not uncommon for people to find their purpose in life after encountering suffering—their own or that of others. The formula involves not only confronting suffering or tragedy but also reflecting on its meaning. It is the power of self-reflection spurred by suffering that can lead to identifying one's life purpose. The alchemy of self-reflection is tremendously potent.

Self-reflection is not to be confused with narcissistic absorption in me and mine, what I think and what I do. It's not "selfie thinking." Rather, self-reflection is thoughtful introspection that enables patterns to be revealed between behavior (cause) and consequence (effect). When we see how our actions can cause suffering to others and even to ourselves, our psychology starts to change. Because it is true that all actions are intertwined in a cause-and-effect web, "Know thyself" is wisdom that was handed down from ancient Greek culture.

Our self-image is a filter for how we see the world. Given this, we can only know the outside world with any certainty and truth when we first gain an appreciation of our own inner world. Introspection is at the foundation of many Eastern philosophies and meditative practices. Meditation offers a way to know the self and, in doing so, to know others. It is a form of contemplative wisdom. When we can see deeply into what is going on, we become a potential change-maker, able to transform ourselves and transform situations for the better.

Every life has a measure of sorrow. Sometimes it is this that awakens us.

—BUDDHA

After witnessing tragedy and the consequences of suffering, some people are inspired to become a change agent in the world. Alleviating suffering becomes their purpose. Such is the case with a Colombian man, Jaime Jaramillo, whose gracious and unrelenting acts of caregiving for street orphans have built his reputation as a national hero. The people of Colombia lovingly refer to him as "Papá Jaime."[6] Papa found his sense of purpose after witnessing the death of a seven-year-old homeless girl.

It was Christmas 1973 when he saw a truck turn the corner and a box, the empty packaging for a doll, was casually tossed out the window and landed in the middle of the street. He watched the young girl sprint toward it to pick it up. Wishing for a Christmas gift of her own, the girl became so immersed in retrieving the box in which she hoped to find a doll that she was oblivious to the large truck heading toward her at full speed. As Papá Jaime watched in helpless horror, the child, clutching the box, was killed instantly. As she died, the girl was smiling, looking directly into Papá Jaime's eyes. In an instant, he was forever changed. In that moment, he realized, *I have to help these children. This is my calling.*

After witnessing this tragedy, Papá Jaime set about helping homeless children who were forced to fend for themselves in the chaotic streets of Bogotá. He witnessed the injustices and abuse they endured. He visited them, making sure they had a meal and caring for them in whatever way he could.

When he embarked on this effort, the practice was for fancy restaurant owners and other businesspeople to call the police to remove what they called "trash kids" from the sidewalks near their establishments. They thought it was bad for business to have such "trash" near their doorways. Like a death squad, the police would arrive and brutalize the children, sometimes burning or killing them. Papa saw that society did not recognize these children as having rights, that they were considered disposable, without value. He began helping these children with burns and other injuries, saving their lives. Papá Jaime made this his life's purpose.

He embarked on this path without any sense of how many lives he would eventually enrich. He said, "I didn't care if I helped one child or one thousand children. What was important to me was that the little girl or boy would be able to expand their conscience and find their internal light in such darkness." Initially, Papá Jaime had no idea where the children came from, where they went, or where they slept. Eventually, he asked a child to escort him into the subculture of the sewers, where hundreds and even thousands huddled in fear and darkness under the streets. He desired to bring every one of them out of the darkness—literally—into the light. Papá Jaime vowed to press on with his work until there were no more children left abandoned in the streets and sewers.

And he did. Papá Jaime has devoted his life to housing, feeding, clothing, and schooling children in need. As the years passed, he gained skills and resources to help children with disease, disabilities, and drug addictions. He enlisted the help of others and expanded his sphere of influence. Over time, his actions shifted the thinking of those Colombian business owners who once called the police to remove the children. Today they call him to help the children. Known as the "father of untouchables," Papá Jaime has educated more than thirty-two thousand Colombian orphans. Some of these children are now successful professionals—computer scientists, teachers, doctors, and athletes.

It is not uncommon for people to find their purpose in life after encountering suffering—their own or that of others. The formula involves not only confronting suffering or tragedy but also reflecting on its meaning. It is the power of self-reflection spurred by suffering that can lead to identifying one's life purpose.

Papá Jaime also operates a renowned leadership organization that teaches people about compassion, service, and peacebuilding. Many of the young adults he helped now give back to support the organization. From one young girl's tragedy came hope and help for many thousands of children. At the hub of that transformation was a man faithfully living his purpose.

Sanjiv Chopra met Papá Jaime at a leadership conference several years ago, and they have since become friends. This friendship offers a personal window into Papá Jaime's amazing—at times, even miraculous—work.

One photo Papá Jaime shared was especially unforgettable, one of his "kids." The young man was the Colombian junior national champion of tennis. He was immaculately dressed in white and was flanked by two superstars in the tennis world, Pete Sampras and Andre Agassi. His star has risen.

"I didn't care if I helped one child or one thousand children. What was important to me was that the little girl or boy would be able to expand their conscience and find their internal light in such darkness."—Papá Jaime

---

One young girl was on the verge of death after suffering police-inflicted third-degree burns when Papá Jaime found her. He gave her shelter and took care of her as she healed. A bright girl, she quickly began excelling in her studies. Eventually, she came to the United States on a computer science scholarship and is now a mother back in her home country of Colombia, working and thriving. Papá Jaime says that her son plays with his own biological grandson. "They are both my grandsons!" he beams.

Sanjiv once asked Papá Jaime how he supports his mission.

"Oh, the money comes. It just comes," Papá Jaime said.

"How? What do you mean that it just comes?" Sanjiv inquired.

Bake sales provide 50 percent of the funding. Some of the organization's staff make cookies, and Papa has convinced many restaurant and shop owners in Bogotá to put a cookie jar beside the cash register. Customers can help themselves to the cookies and pay whatever they wish. Skeptics laughed when Papa began this cookie jar fund-raising in places such as Bogotá, because honor systems there are nonexistent. Yet it works.

"But where do you get the rest of the money?" Sanjiv pressed.

Papa is a renowned international motivational speaker. He gives his entire speaking honoraria to the foundation.

"But that can't possibly cover all your expenses, can it?" Sanjiv asked.

"Oh," Papa replied with a grin, "the rest of the money just comes to me." He told of once needing $41,000 to cover operational expenses. As he was returning from the bank after a disappointing meeting with a loan manager who had denied his request for the funding, he happened upon a homeless woman whom he recognized. She ran up to hug him, and he asked if she was hungry. Papa invited her to his office for coffee and cookies. While the woman was in his office, a call came in about another pending loan request, so Papá Jaime excused himself to take the call. The woman overheard the conversation and sensed the call was not going well.

When Papá Jaime returned, she said to him, "If you need money, I'll give it to you."

Papa smiled gently and clarified that it was a large sum of money—$41,000.

"No problem," the woman replied. "Here. Have it! You need it. Your children need it. I'll give it to you. You can pay it back later if you want, or you don't have to pay it back at all. No questions asked."

She opened her bag and pulled out a wad of cash totaling $60,000. It turns out that her son had been sending her money to get her off the street. She wholeheartedly insisted that he take the money.

And so, just like that, the money comes.

Papa is truly a blessed man. About three years ago, Papa had a hang gliding accident. As he was gliding, he was heading in the direction of some wires, and he urgently had to steer away from them, which caused him to crash violently into a tree. Sanjiv got word that Papa was in the hospital and called to speak with his friend who had been transferred to the neurosurgical ICU.

Papa said, "Oh, I'm fine. I seemed to have lost my sense of smell, but all of my other senses are wonderfully heightened!"

Sanjiv thought he sounded a little ungrounded and euphoric and asked if he was on steroids. He was trying to assess if Papa was thinking clearly. Papa assured him that everything was just fine.

"But you almost died today, Papa!" Sanjiv said.

"But I didn't. I couldn't die. I have to be here for my kids and grandkids."

How extraordinary is the person who has such a will to live because of the passion found every day in living a life of purpose.

El Sistema[7] is a system for elevating children born into poverty, a common reference for the National System of Youth and Children's Orchestras of Venezuela. It was founded by a man whose background did not foretell his trajectory as a leader in music education. José Antonio Abreu earned his doctorate in petroleum economics and began his career in politics. When he became disillusioned with politics, he devoted his life to music, and that decision changed youth culture and the economics in his home country of Venezuela. His life became a symphony of service.

In living this change that he wanted to see in the world, Abreu the economist became a student again—a student of the piano and musical composition. Following his heart, he was determined that music would be a vehicle of social change. As he became musically literate, Abreu the economist began morphing into Abreu the activist.

Abreu's work began with eleven students learning classical music in an underground parking garage in Caracas. He took children off the street and began teaching them the lessons of music: harmony, cooperation, solidarity, compassion, and discipline. Music allows for the deepest expression of human emotion, conveying what words alone cannot. In learning to articulate this elegant and expressive language, these youths—with musical instruments in hand—shape their own brighter futures.

In Abreu's view, the symphony represents a microcosm of an ideal society. The work of El Sistema is to reshape society by teaching social values through music. As with Papá Jaime's kids, the young boys and girls at El Sistema came from crushing poverty, and their futures were not promising. Participation in the El Sistema is free, but it requires diligent work; the students train and rehearse for four hours every single day after school.

Parents from the barrios, or slums, are eager to enroll their children and place them on waiting lists that can last for years, but each one finds that it is worth the wait, because they witness the transformation that occurs in the El Sistema students and understand that it offers a way out of the barrios.

As performers around the globe, the children see the world. Once when a group of El Sistema youth musicians performed at the Vienna Philharmonic, critics hailed it as the performance of the year. From the street to the symphony hall, what a lesson in achievement. As Plato said, "Music is a moral law. It gives soul to the universe, wings to the mind, flight to the imagination, and charm and gaiety to life and to everything."

Abreu has received a series of awards over the years for his work—honorary degrees, a Right Livelihood Award, TED Prize,[8] honors from the World Economic Forum, and global music recognition from many sources, including from the organization that grants the Latin Grammy Award. In accepting one of these many awards, Abreu spoke of the mission of El Sistema: "In the struggle for human rights, let us vigorously incorporate children's sublime right to music, in whose bosom shines Beingness in its splendor and its ineffable mystery. Let us reveal to our children the beauty of music and music shall reveal to our children the beauty of life."

To date, more than two million children worldwide have studied in the El Sistema program. Operating about three hundred community music schools called *nucleos*, El Sistema has a long track record of public funding and government support, spanning several government administrations.

Interestingly, the quest for human excellence crosses partisan lines in Venezuela, and music is the vehicle, because El Sistema crosses all political parties. While a handful of El Sistema graduates have become elite musicians of international acclaim—most notably, famed conductor Gustavo Dudamel, now leading both the Los Angeles Philharmonic and the Simón Bolívar Symphony Orchestra of Venezuela[9]—not every child aspires to be a career musician.

For most of the children, music serves another purpose; it becomes a path to excellence and a way to learn what can be achieved through focus and dedication. In this way, music is an entry to another world. And the world, of course, is changed one child at a time.

This Venezuelan symphony has reverberated not only music but also social change—and it all began with one man finding his purpose.

Never doubt that a small group of thoughtful, committed citizens can change the world. Indeed, it is the only thing that ever has.

—MARGARET MEAD

Young people can find their purpose and lead in exemplary ways; Jennifer Staple-Clark, a woman with uncommon vision, is one such example. She has long seen beyond present circumstances and envisions herself as a change-maker, inciting others to improve the lot of people around the world. Her passion and life purpose began to take form in her university dorm room years earlier.

As a nineteen-year-old premed student at Yale University, Jennifer was disheartened to learn of people going blind around the world from preventable and treatable conditions. Their only obstacle to treatment was access to health care. Jennifer was dismayed that poor people did not have access to a doctor when they most needed it. She thought such barriers to basic health were unjust and that people were needlessly suffering, so she resolved to do something about it.

Jennifer assembled thirty fellow students to volunteer in coordinating efforts at a soup kitchen and at a public library in New Haven, Connecticut. Their shared goal was to enable those who were economically disadvantaged to get appropriate and affordable eye care from local ophthalmologists. Within a few months, their work quickly expanded throughout the country and took root in twenty-five university chapters in North American universities. Harnessing this momentum, Jennifer launched a nonprofit organization, Unite for Sight Global Impact Fellows,[10] to bring to bear financial resources and medical personnel to train local doctors in poor regions and to provide eye health care for all regardless of their economic situation.

Unite for Sight supports village eye doctors by training them in global health and effective eye care delivery. This model transforms local eye doctors into highly respected community leaders. On-site care is delivered to those off the beaten path in the countryside as well as to those who live within congested slums. The medical team distributes eyeglasses and medications and often brings individuals with cataracts to the local clinic for surgery. Since its formation, Unite for Sight has spurred more than eighty-seven thousand sight-restoring surgeries.

Understanding that local problems call for local solutions, Unite for Sight supports and empowers local health care workers who are already on the ground. Providing high-quality eye health care to nearly two million of the world's poorest people, Unite for Sight's eye care programming currently focuses on resource-poor areas of Ghana, Honduras, and India. Almost ten thousand fellows have been trained and thousands of volunteers are on the ground, including medical and nursing students, web designers, and ophthalmologists who have helped make eye care possible in Ghana, Honduras, India, and numerous other countries. And its reach of the work is expanding every day.

Unite for Sight annually presents a Global Health & Innovation Conference at Yale University. Attendees flock to this landmark public health event from all fifty states and from more than fifty countries around the world. Jennifer's Unite for Sight model has made her an international thought leader and a social entrepreneur of best practices in global public health.[11] She is a leader who is wise in her insistence to carefully measure the outcomes of the organization's efforts, not just the outputs.

To Jennifer, awards come a distant second to the real

rewards—transforming the lives of others—but like Maestro Abreu, Jennifer has been endowed with numerous recognitions. These honors include the John F. Kennedy New Frontier Award and the American Institute of Public Service's 2009 Jefferson Award, which is considered the equivalent to a Nobel Prize for public service. She is just one example of a single inspiration spawning both service in others and an entire global movement. In other words, living in service of something greater than yourself can be contagious.

> *If you're in the luckiest 1 percent of humanity, you owe it to the rest of humanity to think about the other 99 percent.*
>
> —WARREN BUFFETT

Adam Braun began his career in finance, not knowing that it would ultimately take him to some of the poorest places in the world. He worked as an intern at a hedge fund while still a teenager, and it seemed that great fortune would befall this precocious young financial whiz. He studied at Brown University and quickly went on to work for Bain Capital, one of the world's largest private equity firms. He was well on his way to an upper-crust Wall Street career.

But while traveling abroad in 2005, Adam had a chance encounter with a child who completely altered his trajectory—changing it to one that held even greater fortune. From a chance encounter in which Adam met an eight-year-old beggar on a street in India, his life was changed.

Standing on a busy street, Adam struck up a conversation with the young boy. He asked, "If you could have anything, what would you want?"

"A pencil," the boy replied with a smile.

Adam was captivated by the simplicity of that wish. A pencil? Here was a boy who had nothing, yet all he wished for was a simple pencil.

Without hesitating, Adam reached into his pocket and gave the boy his pencil. The boy's face lit up! He was over the moon! The moment sparked a recalibration of Adam's thinking. It was evident that the young boy standing before him yearned for an education. Adam appreciated that education is one life's greatest resources, and while Adam wasn't a teacher, he did know how to manage resources.

He said to himself, *This idea that you can't actually change someone's life—that you're too young or don't have enough money or you're not in a position of power or influence—is ridiculous. It's a broken idea, and it doesn't exist. You can provide one small act to one individual person that can change the trajectory of their life. When I gave this kid my pencil, I could see this curiosity, this spark of creativity, this sense of opportunity that he had never grasped before filling up within him.*

The memory of the young boy whose one wish was to own a pencil haunted Adam. He returned to New York with new eyes and deep resolve. He founded a nonprofit organization called Pencils of Promise[12] with a mere twenty-five dollars. Cleverly and appropriately named, Pencils of Promise self-identifies as a "for-purpose organization." The name reflects a *promise*, which can mean two things: a commitment to a purposeful life and the fulfillment of that which uplifts the spirit. Pencils of Promise holds all of that and more.

With a mission to create a better world through education, Pencils of Promise builds schools and institutes sustainable educational programs in developing countries. To date, they have built more than three hundred schools in Latin America, Africa, and Asia. The scope of their work is now on the order of twenty-four million hours of life-changing education that provides basic reading, writing, and math skills to children.

Adam invests in people, and his role as a social investor has been lauded by *Forbes* and other entrepreneurial publications.[13] Now a thought leader in the global education space, he has presented at the White House, the United Nations, and the Clinton Global Initiative. Like Jennifer Staple-Clark, Adam was also a recipient of the American Institute of Public Service's Jefferson Award (2015). His book, *The Promise of a Pencil: How an Ordinary Person Can Create Extraordinary Change*,[14] debuted on the *New York Times* Best Seller List. A global shaper, Adam regularly speaks at conferences and is a consultant to Fortune 100 companies.

The first school was built and dedicated in honor of Adam's grandmother, Ma. A Holocaust survivor who saw her extended family die in the Auschwitz concentration camp, Ma nevertheless remained a relentless nurturer of the potential in others. Given the tremendously supportive force that she was during Adam's early life, it was a life dream of Adam's to acknowledge her with the school that launched Pencils of Promise. Adam said:

> The best moment in my career was when I sat my grandmother down and I showed her the photos of our very first school, which was dedicated to her and she didn't know. When I showed her the kids and the struc-

ture and the photo of the school sign, she saw her name on it. That was the best and most emotional moment of my career. It's one of the reasons why I believe so much in Pencils of Promise because I know now what it does for children in the developing world, but also the capacity to unite families here, as well. If I could enable that same experience for every single grandchild or child, then I think we will be able to unite a lot of families and educate a lot of children.

By the time she looked at the final picture of the school, both Ma and Adam were hugging and sobbing. They both knew that the extraordinary promise had been realized.

When we give cheerfully and accept gratefully, everyone is blessed.

—MAYA ANGELOU

Like the example provided by Ma, we live according to the values of the people we surround ourselves with. For young Muhammad Yunus growing up in East Bengal, every day those values were modeled by a hardworking and generous mother. Although Muhammad's mother, Sufia Khatun, knew great hardship—for example, five of her fourteen children died in infancy—she never failed to help others. Poor people would knock on the door of her home when in need, and Sufia never turned a single person away. This kindness had a huge impact on young Muhammad, and he vowed to devote his life to eradicating such crippling poverty. But as often happens, there was an incubation period in which the *how* of carrying out one's life purpose had to percolate, becoming clearer and tangible over time.

Years later, as an economics professor in Bangladesh, Muhammad was leading his students on a field trip when he came upon a poor woman who made bamboo stools for a living. As he interviewed her, he learned that she was borrowing money to buy the raw bamboo material to make the stools. It was stressful to pay off these loans that sometimes came with interest as high as 10 percent per week. The excessive expense left her with merely pennies in profit at the end of each month.

For all her labor, she was earning about two cents a day. Muhammad quickly crunched the numbers in his head. Getting a break in the form of a more favorable interest rate could be a life changer for her, moving the stool maker from stressful subsistence work to having a financial cushion for her business and her family.

Muhammad started to question the very thing he had been teaching, the existing economic models. Like Adam, a self-professed ordinary person, Muhammad took matters into his own hands and started issuing what has now become known as microloans. Out of his own pocket, he loaned money to forty-two basket weavers. On his end, it was a manageable amount of money to loan, but on the receiving side, the funds landed with great weight. These basket weavers changed their psychology, their livelihood, and their lives using Muhammad's microloans. Each loan recipient invested the money in making her basket weaving a sustainable enterprise. Muhammad was hooked.

Although his economic colleagues and bankers were discouraging him, Muhammad kept issuing loans and changing lives. In 1983, he formed the Grameen Bank,[15] which translates into *village bank*, a financial institution based on principles of trust and solidarity. He had created the first social entrepreneurial banking system, and his intuition of trusting the loan recipients was spot-on. A full 97 percent of the loans are repaid in full. Of the loan recipients, 97 percent were women who played a huge role in using the Grameen funds to elevate the quality of life for their entire family. The Grameen model has been replicated in banks throughout the world. In Bangladesh alone, the Grameen Bank has more than 2,500 branches that disperse funds to grassroots entrepreneurs who would never qualify for a traditional bank loan. These bank branches serve more than eight million borrowers in more than 81,000 villages. More than $2 billion in loans have been dispersed and repaid. The ripple effect of this people-powered capital is extraordinary.

Muhammad and the Grameen Bank were joint recipients of the 2006 Nobel Peace Prize. The Norwegian Nobel Committee commended his "efforts through microcredit to create economic and social development from below," and went on to say that "lasting peace cannot be achieved unless large population groups find ways in which to break out of poverty" and that Muhammad and Grameen's work have shown how "even the poorest of the poor can work to bring about their own development." Muhammad has also been honored with the United States Presidential Medal of Freedom and the Congressional Gold Medal.

How do you define your life purpose? We think finding it and living it are the keys to happiness. Personally, this is how we have come to define our own life purpose.

To fulfill my dharma to teach medicine, leadership, and happiness and to do this grounded in humility and with an ardent desire to learn every single day. To treasure with gratitude my family, friends, colleagues, and students who inspire me in countless ways, and, in some small measure, to inspire everyone that I encounter during this amazing life journey.

—Sanjiv

To pay attention to this precious world in which we live for such a brief time, to use the light that is our life to radiate kindness, to learn and to use that knowledge to illuminate the darkness, to appreciate, to forgive, and to be grateful.

—Gina

What is *your* own living purpose? There are exercises to help you illuminate this and examples of the life purpose of others later in the book.

What does it take to become a purpose-driven leader? These stories are not anomalies; they reflect a pattern. Every individual is a member of a new generation of for-purpose social entrepreneurs who are changing the world in ways big and small, and each one began the journey by identifying a life purpose. Each one lives with a purpose that is loving and selfless.

It turns out that purpose-driven leadership has recently become a popular focus of academic research. Authors Nick Craig and Scott A. Snook themselves have a purpose: they are working to help executives find the spark of their own individual lives. They train leaders to be authentic and to figure out their passion and put it to work.

> *Those who are happiest are those who do the most for others.*
> —BOOKER T. WASHINGTON, *UP FROM SLAVERY*

Craig and Snook define leadership purpose as "who you are and what makes you distinctive." They have dubbed their method the purpose-to-impact process and are documenting how adopting that mind-set—living life in alignment with purpose—can build personal resilience and help organizations navigate all manner of growing pains and unexpected storms. Purpose is not a line on your résumé. It goes far beyond *what* you do; it is also *how* you do it and, importantly, *why* you do it. Craig and Snook's invitation to live life with purpose is a reminder that being authentic means simply being yourself. The way to become an extraordinary leader is to know yourself.

Scott Snook loves to talk about ways in which it is possible to live with purpose. His focus is on developing a leadership statement that reflects your purpose rather than your career goal. He believes that family and outside interests are not external to a career but should be incorporated within it. Snook and Craig recommend creating a three- to five-year plan and working backward from there, setting goals for one year, six months, three months, and thirty days.

People whose lives are guided by a purpose are healthier and happier. This is reinforced by one of the longest-running psychology studies in history, the Grant Study. A total of 268 men have been tracked from their college days beginning in the 1930s through the present day. It has become one of the largest longitudinal studies to measure physical and emotional health.

Some of the men went on to have prominent careers, most notably, President John F. Kennedy, whose personal data will remain confidential through 2040. This study has enabled researchers to explore the interrelationships of the variables that separate a meaningful and fulfilling life from one that is less successful. George Vaillant has directed the study for four decades. When asked by a journalist to sum up the results, he said it was quite easy to distill into just one sentence: "Happiness is love—full stop."[16] Living with love is the path to happiness.

The stories told here certainly inspire, but don't let them intimidate. Who can equal these achievements? While some will equal or possibly surpass these extraordinary feats, for the rest, even if one single life is changed by your life's purpose, it will more than suffice and leave the world a better place.

"Three Gratitudes"
Carrie Newcomer

Every night before I go to sleep
I say out loud
Three things that I'm grateful for,
All the significant, insignificant
Extraordinary, ordinary stuff of my life.
It's a small practice and humble,
And yet, I find I sleep better
Holding what lightens and softens my life
Ever so briefly at the end of the day.
Sunlight, and blueberries,
Good dogs and wool socks,
A fine rain,
A good friend,
Fresh basil and wild phlox,
My father's good health,
My daughter's new job,
The song that always makes me cry,
Always at the same part,
No matter how many times I hear it.
Decent coffee at the airport,
And your quiet breathing,
The stories you told me,
The frost patterns on the windows,
English horns and banjos,
Wood Thrush and June bugs,

The smooth glassy calm of the morning pond,
An old coat,
A new poem,
My library card,
And that my car keeps running
Despite all the miles.
And after three things,
More often than not,
I get on a roll and I just keep on going,
I keep naming and listing,
Until I lie grinning,
Blankets pulled up to my chin,
Awash with wonder
At the sweetness of it all.

5

Gratitude as an Anchor

If the only prayer you say in your life is thank you, that would suffice.

—MEISTER ECKHART

The word *gratitude* is derived from the Latin word *gratia*, meaning *grace*. A life filled with grace equates to a life lived with gratitude. A heart expands with gratitude, and it culminates in a reservoir of buoyancy. This leads to resilience, and, as myriad studies have shown, gratitude is a direct path to happiness and even longevity. And happiness, as we well know, is anchored by a life of purpose. A happy and grateful person effortlessly radiates goodness toward others and enriches the lives of those around them.

The experiences that can redirect the course of your life are lightning-strike moments. They are always unplanned, unforgettable, and instantly transformative.

Since it is impossible to plan for these transformational moments, are there things that one can do in their stead to identify a life of purpose? Chief among our conscious acts is to consider how to grapple with difficult times, mine them for meaning, and learn the lessons of resilience.

There is no stronger antidote to experiences that threaten to break us than to reach for gratitude. The good news is that it is possible to cultivate a deep sense of gratitude through intentional action. In other words, the ability to feel gratitude is under our control no matter what the external circumstances.

Gratitude can be developed and nurtured in small steps. It takes root as we make small daily choices to remember the good to reframe the bad. It is a conscious choice. It also is accepting that what we have in the moment is enough. There is a time-honored adage that says "having it all is believing that you already do."

One of the easiest ways to practice gratitude is with the making of a simple list. Wise elders often talk about being grateful for the little things in life. Ask yourself, have you ever taken that advice? Or do you tend to overlook the small stuff in life as being inconsequential? Do you rush by it without notice of all that it can offer?

In essence, the small things in life are just that—small, part of the background. Does the way we view the minutiae of daily life really matter? Could it really hold a key to happiness? If the elders say that the keys to happiness are right in front of us, it is probably worth a listen! Try listening for the small, subtle signals in life, these tiny moments that can illuminate. They can build us up and serve as an antidote for the hardships. As Andy Rooney said, "I've learned that it's those small daily happenings that make life so spectacular."

Have you considered that your present life circumstances are not a roadblock to happiness? The challenges you face may, in fact, be a direct path toward it. Even the roughest experiences that people navigate—divorce, betrayal, the loss of a loved one, bankruptcy, foreclosure of a home, depression—do not eclipse the basic life-giving positives that surround us all the time. If nothing else, they are starting points. Ironically, being at rock bottom can be the *perfect* way to cultivate happiness—but only if you use that experience to cultivate gratitude.

Try listening for the small, subtle signals in life, these tiny moments that can illuminate. They can build us up and serve as an antidote for the hardships.

Let's look at this more systematically. There is a recipe for creating a gratitude list as an ongoing, resilience-building practice. Helen Russell, a spiritual creative and author from New Zealand, has written eloquently about how to do it.[1]

Step one in creating a gratitude list is simply to commit to making a list as a daily practice. Consistency is the important element in obtaining full benefit from the practice. You are beginning a spiritual practice, and it will gain momentum and bear greater fruit as you devote yourself to it. Some days, this may not be easy. Lean into it. Where there is resistance, there is room for growth. When life feels too busy to make a list or too frustrating to search for a tad of gratitude, that is precisely the moment to take a fresh look at your life and begin reframing what you find around you. What goodness you see with those new eyes you must write down on your list.

On the most dreadfully gloomy days, maybe the only thing to feel grateful for is something rather mundane, but that's okay. Helen Russell described how on some days you may only feel able to muster thankfulness for a slice of pizza. And that's okay.

Muster what you can when you can. Begin seeing that the little things are worthy of giving pause, and give thanks for them. Be grateful for the present moment. As Thích Nhất Hạnh has said, "The present moment is the only moment available to us and it is the door to all moments."

The second step is to simply begin. Just get started with your list, knowing that it does not need to be a literary masterpiece. Complete this simple sentence: "I am grateful for _____." Writing it down makes you more conscious of it and make it more real. Writing it down gives it greater gravity than merely thinking about it or talking about it.

Be grateful for small mercies. Tiny good deeds. The sun on your face. Your clean laundry. Whatever comes to mind. And if nothing comes to mind, say, "I am grateful to be alive."

Treat the expression of gratitude as a ritual, a daily practice, which means committing to making your list every single day. Find a time of day in your schedule to do this and protect that time. Treat it seriously, and the gratitude you honor will pay you back many times over. Keep the momentum going. The benefits will only increase.

Begin seeing that the little things are worthy of giving pause and giving thanks for them. Be grateful for the present moment. As Thích Nhất Hạnh has said, "The present moment is the only moment available to us and it is the door to all moments."

As you continue the practice, begin seeing where your gratitude can expand from the discrete moments that you are writing in your gratitude journal to an awareness that becomes peppered throughout your day. You may want to consider finding a gratitude partner. You will help keep each other on track, and it will be fun to watch each other's gratitude list grow.

The Greater Good Science Center in Berkeley encourages

consistency in the practice of keeping a gratitude journal.[2] Consistency is much more important than overthinking it. Keep it simple. Their advice is to list at least five simple things you have experienced that you feel grateful for. This list can be so simple that it may include waking up or your favorite Rolling Stones song. That's enough. It is helpful to remember to focus on people more than things. Be sincere—this project is for you, not to impress anyone else. Don't just go through the motions; think about what you are writing down.

Also, include on your list what your life would be like *without* certain things. In other words, don't just be grateful for what is there, such as lack of illness or absence of rain. Recognize how the absence of certain things makes life better. Finally, realize that the concrete act of writing these gratitude-filled things down has a much stronger impact than just saying them. Your reflection emphasizes the meaning of daily events of your life. Making a list puts the events into a richer context and facilitates integration into your days.

Gratitude consists of feelings and behaviors that acknowledge goodness. Gratitude reinforces that there continually are renewable sources of good, and it teaches this to others.[3]

You may be thinking that this is overthinking the practice. Yes, yes, it is. Because gratitude is a serious life skill, cultivating gratitude is so important that it can change your life. When you begin to see gratitude all around you—when you radiate it from within—you find that there is always something to appreciate. Think of the practice of gratitude as a reframing of the world, and know that it is an advanced life skill[4] that will transform your life.

A committed gratitude practice retrains your brain to see

and respond to the world. It is a training process not unlike how you prepare yourself to run a marathon. Like mining for gold, you'll find yourself looking for the good in yourself and in other people, and looking for the positives in every situation.

You are honing your perceptions. As you practice gratitude, the people around you will fall into one of two camps: either they will mirror back and magnify positives, or they will complain about what is lacking in their life. They, too, are framing their world. We each can choose: Is the world full of simple pleasures or is it full of traffic jams and headaches?

Surrounding yourself with those who always have a kind word to say reinforces your tendency to notice the little wonders of life. Surrounding yourself with those who dwell on negatives will, in effect, be like a leak in your gratitude reservoir.

James Rohn said that we are the average of the five people we spend the most time with. Therefore, choose your friends wisely. Cultivate positive friendships by telling people around you exactly what you appreciate about them. Say "thank you" liberally. You'll be surprised at how relationships can develop in new ways when you openly express gratitude. Finally, if and when negative talk arises, exercise your right to transform the conversation by offering a positive perspective, and if that doesn't work, leave the conversation.

In addition to choosing the company you keep, it is also important to be selective about the media that you consume. News channels can be a negative bombardment of information. Talk about a drain on your gratitude reservoir. Reading the news can convince you that everything in the world is in trouble, bad, sad, negative. There are ways to keep a positive focus. You want to be informed of what is happening in the world, but ration it in small doses so that it doesn't reverse the benefits of your gratitude practice.

Cultivating gratitude is so important that it can change your life. When you begin to see gratitude all around you—when you radiate it from within—you find that there is always something to appreciate. Think of the practice of gratitude as a reframing of the world and know that it is an advanced life skill that will transform your life.

If your starting point is that you really don't know what to express gratitude for—if it is not arising naturally and announcing itself like an eager first grader waiting to be called on by teacher—welcome the art of faking it until you make it. If gratitude doesn't feel real at first, behave as if it is real, and it will become real. This is one reason that consistency is key. Faking it, or taking small steps in the right direction, really does produce results in the intended direction.

For instance, smiling for twenty seconds, even if you don't feel like it, has been shown to increase happiness.[5] Smiling changes our physiology to start with, and then the effect extends outward, spreading happiness to others. Smiling and gratitude can improve the environment that you're in! Smile at others and tell them what you're grateful for—little by little, you're changing yourself and you're changing the world.

Gratitude is a choice. The expression of gratitude is a choice.

SCIENCE OF GRATITUDE

Let's dig a little deeper into the research that supports gratitude as a practice and the benefits it can have on your daily life.

Robert Emmons is a psychology professor at the University of California–Davis and is considered one of the foremost experts on gratitude in the world.[6] He calls gratitude the "forgotten factor in happiness research." Highlights of his research are distilled here. In a nutshell, his careful research shows that gratitude produces real results in the body, in the mind, and in the social world.

Expressing gratitude has been shown to improve physical health. Specifically, writing in a gratitude journal at least weekly correlates with more time spent exercising and fewer complaints about aches and pains. This is in comparison to those who wrote in a journal about life's negative events.

A gratitude practice also is associated with higher energy, alertness, and determination, which results in a greater capacity to achieve one's goals. In fact, in adults with neuromuscular disease, a three-week gratitude practice resulted in better sleep and higher energy levels.

When we express gratitude, the brain shifts in positive ways. We learn and remember more effectively, as evidenced by improved scores on academic tests. We give up the tendency to play the victim or feel entitlement, and we expand our capacity to deal with tragedy.

Interestingly, while a gratitude practice is correlated with experiencing pleasant emotions, it does not significantly dissipate negative emotions. In other words, grateful people are fully aware of the negativity around them. They simply choose not to focus on it, and in doing so, they experience a higher level of life satisfaction.

When we choose to see life through a lens of gratitude, the benefits are far reaching. With gratitude, we shift things for the collective and produce real social change. Our relationships improve, and we experience a richer sense of community. Gratitude leads to more social activity and a desire to make contact with others, to spend more time with them. Individuals with a gratitude practice are more likely to respect and honor the interconnectedness of life and are more likely to share with others and to feel responsibility toward them. Gratitude leads to greater empathy, to a better understanding of others, to feeling less envy, and to a reduced focus on material things.

Because of this, gratitude is the very best practice we can share with our children. As you consider the list of scientifically proven gifts of gratitude,[7] you will see that these are lifelong gifts that you want to share with your children as well as with all your loved ones.

Seven Gifts of Gratitude
1. More relationships and more meaningful relationships
2. Better physical health and habits of self-care
3. Better mental health and less negative emotion
4. Increased empathy and reduced aggression
5. Regular, more restful sleep
6. Increased self-esteem and reduced social envy
7. Greater resistance to trauma

You see, gratitude is a social gift—it expands as you share it. Gratitude makes us appreciate others' successes, rather than feel threatened or inferior to them. Gratitude enables us to build a meaningful support network for those around us.

THE SCIENCE OF GRATITUDE

Neurologist Oliver Sacks has been called the most famous brain scientist in the world. A personable scholar, he has been said to put a human face on the science of the mind. He was a weaver of compelling adventure stories, which can be thought of as case studies, that grabbed your attention. For example, he wrote *The Man Who Mistook His Wife for a Hat and Other*

Clinical Tales. He had a unique knack of capturing medical details with great heart. The book is a collection of essays that were originally published for *The New York Times.* In its own way, the book is a masterpiece.

When Oliver Sacks made a public announcement that he was nearing the end of his life, he began writing about gratitude, specifically the gratitude he felt at being afforded unexpected extra years following his initial cancer diagnosis.

Before he was a famous author, Sacks was a boy with a troubled childhood, but that led him to grow into a man with a strong sense of empathy. As we know, empathy is one step away from compassion, and Sacks became one of the most compassionate medical writers of our time.

Sacks's brilliant words lift us up:

> My predominant feeling is one of gratitude. I have loved and been loved; I have been given much and I have given something in return. . . . Above all, I have been a sentient being, a thinking animal, on this beautiful planet, and that in itself has been an enormous privilege and adventure.[8]

Where in your day do you find privilege and adventure? And who is there with you to appreciate and share it? Every day, for just one moment, pause and look around. Gratitude is waiting for you. Adventure and joy are waiting for you. They surround you, at work, at home, in play, and in all relationships. You must keep an eye open and reach out for them.

"My predominant feeling is one of gratitude. I have loved and been loved; I have been given much and I have given something in return. . . . Above all, I have been a sentient being, a thinking animal, on this beautiful planet, and that in itself has been an enormous privilege and adventure."—Oliver Sacks

---

Sacks was a role model who showed how gratitude can lead to a life that ends with grace. He chose not to fight the cancer when it became inevitable. Rather, he accepted it. At the end, even as he was on his way to death, he continued to be filled up by life.

Grateful people grow old and die with greater ease. According to Sacks, days spent expressing thanks acknowledge our incompleteness in the most wonderful of ways. He didn't mean incomplete because something is lacking but rather incomplete in that there is room for the world to fill us up. There is an old Leonard Cohen song with lyrics to help us make this point:

There is a crack in everything. That's how the light gets in.

GRATITUDE IN THE WORKPLACE

Search high and low and you may not find a better work culture than Google. The Google goal is "to create the happiest, most productive workplace in the world." What are their strategic methods for doing so? They are all based on giving and on unconventional perks that spark and maintain motivation. The net effect appears to be working. Google employees rate the company very favorably. Also, the Great Place to Work Institute and *Fortune* honored Google in 2014 as the "Best Company to Work For." What can we learn from Google in terms of making gratitude a pillar of group culture?

Google has created a culture for their employees that taps into what we'll call the four Fs: flexibility, freedom, fun, and food. These factors create an environment where employees can focus their talents on their work, resulting in their most creative and aspirational work. Their energy then can be spent advancing their potential instead of burning a lot of cognitive energy and emotion on the more basic day-to-day chores and constraints.[9]

Flexibility extends to work hours (optimizing timing for individual peak performance), work processes, and attire—in a nutshell, their workers are working when and how they are most comfortable.

Freedom offers the opportunity for employees to work on anything employees want for 20 percent of their time. Gmail, for example, was a product of this 20 percent rule.

Fun is built into the workplace and culture through interior space design, company events, and things like silly costume days. At Google, participating in something fun is an expected everyday part of the culture.

Food is provided—meal options and free snacks—to support employee health. A Google rule is that employees are never more than 150 feet away from food, entirely avoiding the hassle of planning and packing meals in advance.

In effect, Google leaders do what they can to show employees that they are grateful for their contributions. Such appreciation goes a long way in having employees bring their A game. They understand that great ideas cannot be forced and that the best way to cultivate great ideas is to continually show gratitude for the talent that people bring.

Thinking of the world-changing products that this company has built, just imagine how the effects of gratitude can scale and how it is changing the world as we know it.

GRATITUDE IN MARRIAGE

What are the words that come to mind when you think of gratitude? *Recognized? Acknowledged? Appreciated? Valued? Treasured?* These are some of the words that pave a pathway leading to happiness in long-term relationships—especially marriage. If you think of marriage as a special bond, even a sacred bond, it is no wonder that gratitude plays an important role in the vitality of a marriage. What better way to love and honor someone than with a daily heart of gratitude?

Gratitude begets more gratitude. It not about idealism. It's practical. Expressing appreciation to your spouse generates similar feelings that are mirrored back. This reciprocal appreciation lifts the relationship. It works against the inertia of the downward spiral that some long-term relationships sadly experience, where one or both partners begin to ignore in each other the special qualities that made them fall in love in the first place. We have all heard the stories. We see this stereotype played out in movies and on television. Nagging and annoyed spouses are presented to us as comedies, but in life they are not funny.

It is far better to laugh together. Laughing with joy makes the bond better and stronger over the years. This is not to say that the honeymoon phase will last forever, but gratitude will deepen the bond. Reciprocal appreciation has been shown to hold relationships together longer.[10] It produces a stronger commitment for a longer time.

So, how do we express gratitude to our spouses? It seems to be more in what we do than in what we say. Gratitude is felt when we lean in to the conversation, giving the other person our full attention. We make eye contact and respond. We use physical affection. Touch goes a long way toward expressing appreciation. Touch releases oxytocin, the bonding hormone.

Reciprocal appreciation amplifies trust and respect. It creates the supportive scaffolding for the relationship where it is easy and natural to feel needed and valued. It creates enduring connection. As we all know, relationships are dynamic. They change over time and constantly involve give-and-take, so creating connection and increasing velocity in a relationship is a direction (upward) with momentum (onward) fueled by gratitude.

Gratitude is the catalyst for all that is good in a relationship!

If you are married or in a long-term relationship and want to stoke the velocity of gratitude, know that it begins with you. Take the initiative and commit to a practice of complimenting your partner every day. Every day write a short note or send an email to your partner that expresses gratitude. You will find the dividends are remarkable. Focus on your communication skills, and be a little more generous with touch. Stay calm when there is conflict, and use every opportunity to build collaboration and make decisions together. It will make a tremendous difference over time.

And if you are single, find the beauty and goodness in the people around you. It might be a kind word to the taxi driver, the waiter, your boss, or your lonely neighbor. You will create ripples of goodness in your community, and the side effect is that you are in training to become the future partner that you desire—one who sees the good and amps up the momentum of gratitude and happiness.

RAISING GRATEFUL CHILDREN

Parenting expert Patty Onderko shared a meaningful how-to article on the ways in which a caregiver can raise grateful child.[11] Recognizing that it is an ongoing process and that role modeling the behavior ourselves is one of the most potent things to reinforce the child's learning, here is a list of strategies that help us teach gratitude in the little teachable daily moments that Onderko suggests:

- Teach your children that what they want is not always what they will get. Let them know that while you appreciate them asking for things that they want, they should never expect to get it all.
- Encourage your children to express out loud what it is they like about gifts they receive to help them make connections with what they are given. Teach them to pause and see value.
- Allow your child to be part of the process of buying things for others.
- Teach them to appreciate experiences, not stuff.
- Remember that you are the ultimate role model for the desired behavior.
- Set an example. Always say thank you for everything you receive.

Your child will notice.

Expose children to people of all walks of life so that they appreciate what they have and appreciate all types of people. Teach them to walk in others' shoes.

Reciprocal appreciation amplifies trust and respect. It creates the supportive scaffolding for the relationship where it is easy and natural to feel needed and valued. It creates enduring connection.

GRATITUDE AT HOLIDAY TIME

Holidays in American culture tend to have a materialistic streak. We can lament that fact, or we can use the holidays to harness the opportunity for gratitude. The *Wall Street Journal* published an article discussing how materialistic thoughts interfere with gratitude and happiness.[12] Materialism tends to generate on negative emotion rather than focus on the most meaningful aspects of life. Money is not inherently evil, of course. While it is not antithetical to happiness, we need to have the discernment to put it in its place and not worship it. Spend on experiences. Money should serve a purpose. The antidote to materialism is the expression of gratitude.

GRATITUDE ACROSS CULTURES

Holidays are culture-specific experiences, of course. It turns out that the expression of gratitude has interesting cross-cultural variations as well. Sean Robertson, an Australian traveling in China, reflected on what stood out to him when he was exposed to Chinese methods of expressing gratitude.[13] In effect, in China gratitude is everywhere, although it is rarely spoken. To say the words *thank you* is not generally comfortable to Chinese individuals. It is perceived as creating distance and formality, so it is rarely used. Politeness is the norm, so gratitude happens through action instead of words.

In China, people ascribe to the way of the *bao*—it is an extreme embodiment of the Golden Rule. The *bao* is inherent in every daily interaction. It is assumed that a good deed is returned in kind—a given that if I do something kind for you, you will return the kindness. Therefore, there is no need to write a thank-you note. Gratitude is demonstrated in behavior, every single day. It is understood that all that is given will one day be reciprocated.

Here's a list of cultural fun facts so you can appreciate how gratitude is expressed in different countries across the globe:

China: "Thank you" is said in gesture, not in words.
Japan: Gratitude is expressed with a bow. Its depth and duration are significant.
Russia and Hungary: Nothing says appreciation like chocolate and flowers, but not yellow flowers, because they are considered bad luck.

Germany: Students express gratitude after a lecture, but instead of clapping, they knock on their desks.

Nepal: In this culture, it is customary to use both hands to both give and receive a gift.[14]

Gratitude is a form of love, so in a related way, it is interesting to see how the expression of love from parent to child differs across cultures. These behaviors form the basis of social norms that determine the happiness quotient of the entire population.

It is critical for children to feel loved and accepted in the context of their culture, and here is what that looks like in countries around the world, courtesy of *The Huffington Post*.

Sweden: In this egalitarian nation, parents show love by treating children as equals.

Philippines: Parents show love by teaching their children to honor their parents by fulfilling family obligations.

Kenya: Love is expressed by strongly controlling children's behavior.

Colombia: Children are taught that family needs are greater than any other personal relationships.

China: A dominant trend is that fathers have recently become more nurturing as traditional gender roles diminish.

Italy: Love is expressed to children through parental involvement and overt, verbal expression of great emotion.

Jordan: Parents constantly adjust the child's behavior to promote physical, mental, social, and spiritual growth.

Thailand: Love is imparted through respect and through traditional Buddhist teachings.

United States: Parents tend to promote their child's individual interests and their freedom to make own choices.[15]

LIFE AS TEACHER

Renowned Buddhist teacher Jack Kornfield teaches in the West, bringing wise lessons from the East along with practices in meditation and compassion.[16] He teaches that in some of the Eastern Buddhist temples, there is a prayer that asks for difficulties: May I be given the appropriate difficulties so that my heart can truly open with compassion.

Kornfield teaches that we should approach life with abundant gratitude, and he teaches how to do just that. He says that a spiritual life does not stop at being grateful for life's blessings; we must also embrace suffering and be thankful for it as an integral component to our spiritual development. The heart will grow wiser and more compassionate when we navigate the turbulence of life as compared to sailing in the still waters of the status quo and peace. Turbulence brings our attention to the moment; it cuts through distraction. A distracted mind is an ungrateful mind.

In his book *A Path with Heart*, he wrote, "This life is a test— it is only a test. If it had been an actual life, you would have received further instructions on where to go and what to do. Remember, this life is only a test."

These notions are not simply spiritual lingo that may work in the monastery but not on Main Street. Research confirms that adversity builds gratitude and resilience. We like to think of gratitude as the anchor for resilience. The Mayo Clinic posted a wonderful summary on its website describing how resilience is the ultimate skill necessary for adaptability.[17] Resilience keeps us functioning despite setbacks; it helps us move beyond challenges, heartbreak, and misfortunes. As we find a deeper source of inner strength, we bounce back. Resilience helps us cope in healthy ways and wards off mental illness.

Are there ways that we can intentionally dive into life training that helps build resilience? An article in *Time* shared a multitude of ways that we can galvanize ourselves toward stronger emotional resilience in order to bounce back from life's challenges.[18] This list is taken from Steven Southwick's book *Resilience: The Science of Mastering Life's Greatest Challenges*. Here are the top ten research-supported ways that to boost emotional resilience:

1. **Be optimistic.** Focus positively on the problems you can solve.
2. **Face your fears.** Avoiding fears strengthens them, but facing them, even for a few moments, allows the brain to weaken the fear connection.
3. **Guide yourself with a moral compass.** A sense of what is right and what is wrong will strengthen your resolve and offer you tools for tough times.

4. **Have a spiritual practice.** This not only benefits you personally, but as a bonus, it benefits and uplifts your entire community.

5. **Use the strength of social support.** Recognize that asking for help is not a weakness.

6. **Surround yourself with positive role models,** or at least recognize negative role models and focus on doing the opposite of what they do.

7. **Get regular exercise.** This is especially important if you are a highly emotional person, because it forces you to tolerate the same physical symptoms of anxiety arousal but without an emotional reaction.

8. **Be a lifelong learner.** Constant learning keeps the brain healthy and sharp and builds overall self-esteem.

9. **Strive for cognitive flexibility.** This flexibility will pay off with multiple routes to solving problems and enable you to cope gracefully with challenging situations.

10. **Find meaning in your life.** Because so much of our time is spent with our work, it is also important that you seek a calling as you find a profession.

Wayne Dyer, best-selling author, philosopher, and motivational speaker, echoes these guidelines when he says we must learn to bend and not break. When a problem comes, see it as an opportunity to learn and test yourself to your deepest abilities. Don't be trapped in a rigid set of rules, and you will grow deeper, stronger roots and become more resilient.

In other words, learn from trees in a storm; those that bend with the wind do not break. Dyer wrote, "Keep an inner vision of the wind symbolizing difficult situations as you affirm: I have no rigidity within me. I can bend to any wind and remain unbroken. I will use the strength of the wind to make me even stronger and better preserved."[19]

We must also embrace suffering and be thankful for it as an integral component to our spiritual development. The heart will grow wiser and more compassionate when we navigate the turbulence of life as compared to sailing in the still waters of the status quo and peace.

The science is clear that resilience can be learned.[20] It all comes down to developing an internal locus of control. Working backward from there, the compass that guides us to an internal locus of control is also under our control. We get to this by repeatedly choosing to focus on the significant meaning of our life experiences, no matter how averse or even traumatic they may be. When a trauma is relabeled in the brain as a meaningful experience, we extract goodness from it. We push our breaking point further out and redefine our sense of adaptability. In this way, resilience is the ultimate life skill.

This message of flexibility and resilience is found in the spiritual teachings of the *Tao Te Ching*:

> Men are born soft and supple; dead, they are stiff and hard. Plants are born tender and pliant; dead, they are brittle and dry.
>
> Thus whoever is stiff and inflexible is a disciple of death. Whoever is soft and yielding is a disciple of life.
>
> The hard and stiff will be broken. The soft and supple will prevail.[21]

Pause for a moment and let the meaning of these wise words resonate. What circumstances in your life make your heart feel hard? What situations induce thinking that is stiff and stuck? Contrast these situations with who you imagine you could be if your emotions, attitudes, and thoughts were flexible and resilient, if they gravitated toward finding the meaningful?

An extreme example of turning trauma into resilience is the story of Celia Henick Feldman, a survivor of the Auschwitz concentration camp. In an interview, she recounted her story of survival as being full of "bittersweet memories," even though she was living in a death camp and starving.[22] In fact, her memoir is titled *Bittersweet Memories*. Her drive to share her story is to educate others so that the loss so many experienced at Auschwitz will not be forgotten.

"Face your fears. Avoiding fears strengthens them, but facing them, even for a few moments, allows the brain to weaken the fear connection."—Steven Southwick

---

Feldman found her purpose—the main ingredient of resilience—through tremendous adversity. Nonetheless, she considers herself the "happiest person on the planet" because of the gifts that have come into her life since then, including her family, her education, and her love for the United States. Feldman's wise words are encouragement to figure out how to do good for others to find happiness for yourself. She says that your life is in your own hands, that there can be an internal sense of control even when outside circumstances appear to exert complete control. She tells us that the heart should always be grateful for struggles.

Countless life stories and research papers have a unanimous conclusion: resilience is a learned trait that is often strengthened when you experience turbulence in your life. Sources of turbulence may include divorce and its aftermath[23] as well as finding the strength to move on after the death of a partner[24] or a child.[25] Building resilience means increasing our ability to take life's blows in stride and press forward.

If you are going through rough times in your life, always remember that resilience is learned and gets stronger with practice, stronger each time it is tested through adversity.[26] A consistent trait of resilient people who have experienced trauma is that they all believed they were in control over their own happiness even if they did not have control over what happened to them. Relationships serve a critical role here because loved ones remind us that optimism still exists.

STUDIES IN FORTITUDE

Ever more people today have the means to live, but no meaning to live for.

—VIKTOR FRANKL

Viktor Frankl, an Austrian psychiatrist and neurologist, survived the death camp of Auschwitz and went on to write one of the most influential books ever written, *Man's Search for Meaning.* At the heart of his message is a profound truth: "In some way, suffering ceases to be suffering at the moment it finds a meaning."

While in the concentration camp, Frankl had an illuminating realization—that despair has the potential to be bottomless, but even from that abyss, one can discover meaning and purpose. He famously wrote, "Everything can be taken from a man but one thing: the last of the human freedoms—to choose one's attitude in any given set of circumstances, to choose one's own way."[27]

Frankl observed that those who found meaning in their dire circumstances survived much longer than those who did not. From this, he also learned that taking responsibility in one's own life is the major factor shaping a person and the ability to be resilient.

Frankl recalled a young woman who knew she would soon be put to death, and he observed that, despite this knowledge, she was resilient and had found meaning during the darkest of days. In fact, he found she was cheerful. Her solace? From her cell, she could see two blossoms on a single branch of a chestnut tree. "This tree here is the only friend I have in my loneliness," she said. "I often talk to the tree . . . it said to me, 'I am here—I am here—I am life, eternal life."

Frankl recounted numerous examples of people who rose above their dire circumstances and chose to help fellow sufferers. Some even gave away their last piece of bread. The lesson he learned and passed to us is that we have the power to choose. We determine how we react to any situation or challenge, and through this choice we can find meaning and purpose.[28]

Another exceptional individual was Christopher Reeve. He could do anything. He was Superman.

We will forever think of the actor Christopher Reeve as the superhero he played so well. Ironically, there are parallels in the lives of the fictional character and the film star. Both had the challenge of facing down physical limitations. In 1995, Reeve had a horseback riding accident and suffered a devastating spinal cord injury that left him a quadriplegic whose every breath was dependent on a respirator.

But Superman Reeve survived and became a symbol of resilience. In his tragedy, he found his life purpose. He established a foundation to improve the lives of those with spinal cord injuries.

But as many who seek their life purpose find, the path is not always straightforward. This was true of Reeve's journey. His wife, Dana Reeve, recounted that there were times he wanted to die, and she would remind him, "You are still you. I love you. Let's not give up." With her help, he persevered and discovered a life-changing purpose. As he so eloquently said, "I'm not living the life I thought I would lead, but it does have meaning, purpose. There is love . . . there is joy . . . there is laughter."

Louie Zamperini, who competed in the 1936 Olympic Games as a runner, enlisted in the United States Army Air Corps at the beginning of World War II and was deployed in the Pacific. He endured the unimaginable when his plane crashed and he survived after being adrift at sea for an unfathomable forty-seven days. He was taken hostage by the Japanese navy, and while at a prisoner of war camp, he became the victim of a sadistic prison commander.

Despite this unrelentingly trauma, Zamperini found a path that enabled him to conquer the trauma and the subsequent PTSD and to rebuild a life noted for forgiveness, service, and peace.

Zamperini's sage wisdom is distilled in these words: I think the hardest thing in life is to forgive. Hate is self-destructive. If you hate somebody, you're not hurting the person you hate, you're hurting yourself. It's a healing, actually, it's a real healing . . . forgiveness.

Sometimes what we see as a loss turns out in the end to be a gain, and sometimes a gain is a loss. I try not to be too swift to pass judgment on any situation, preferring instead to be patient and take the long view because I believe that in the end all things work together for good.

One day we were fighting for our lives, the next we were enjoying the clouds, the sunset, the soaring albatross, the dolphins and porpoises. Through it all I never lost my sense that life could be beautiful. I kept my zest for living, morning and night. I'd made it this far and refused to give up because all my life I had always finished the race.[29]

"Everything can be taken from a man but one thing: the last of the human freedoms—to choose one's attitude in any given set of circumstances, to choose one's own way."—Viktor Frankl

These stories inspire, and they are a reminder that adversity is often a game changer if one is open to reflection, acceptance, and forgiveness. Those who exhibit fortitude will find the gift of resilience when confronting life's hardships.

As has been said by way of conventional wisdom, hardships often prepare those of us who are ordinary people for an extraordinary destiny.

No matter what life throws your way, whether it is disappointments large or small, sorrows that wound your spirit, or unanticipated detours, meet these setbacks with an abundance of gratitude. Find a way to be grateful for the gift of adversity, for the lessons learned and the new paths that open. You don't know where the path may lead, but what is certain is that by cloaking these hardships in gratitude, your heart will be lighter and, in due time, happiness will find you.

"The Ponds"
Mary Oliver

Every year
the lilies
are so perfect
I can hardly believe

their lapped light crowding
the black,
mid-summer ponds.
Nobody could count all of them—

the muskrats swimming
among the pads and the grasses
can reach out
their muscular arms and touch

only so many, they are that
rife and wild.
But what in this world
is perfect?

I bend closer and see
how this one is clearly lopsided—
and that one wears an orange blight—
and this one is a glossy cheek

half nibbled away—
and that one is a slumped purse
full of its own
unstoppable decay.

Still, what I want in my life
is to be willing
to be dazzled—
to cast aside the weight of facts

and maybe even
to float a little
above this difficult world.
I want to believe I am looking

into the white fire of a great mystery.
I want to believe that the imperfections are nothing—
that the light is everything—that it is more than the sum
of each flawed blossom rising and fading. And I do.

6

Daily Practices for a More Purposeful You

The soul is dyed the color of its thoughts. Think only on those things that are in line with your principles and can bear the light of day. The content of your character is your choice. Day by day, what you do is who you become. Your integrity is your destiny—it is the light that guides your way.

—HERACLITUS

FOCUS ON FRIENDSHIPS FOR GREATER LONGEVITY

Growing old together with kindred spirits is one of the most enriching experiences available to human beings. Not only do intimacy and friendship boost happy feelings, but keeping good company can even delay that big solo adventure into the unknown.

Since the 1960s, isolation has been proven to increase the pace of mental decay in old age.[1] Marjorie Lowenthal spearheaded research into the relationship of friendship to longevity and health. Her early work focused on the assumption that living alone can aggravate—or even cause—mental disorders in the elderly. She found that residents of assisted-living homes had worse mental clarity and other problems when they lived in extreme isolation. More recently, people have examined the correlation of friendship with health, longevity, education, adaptation, child-rearing, and business success, to name a few areas of study.

It has long been known there is tremendous benefit to having close friends, but now it even appears that friendships can delay death. According to a study published in 2012, loneliness is a serious health risk factor for those over age sixty. Carla Perissinotto and her peers at the University of California–San Francisco set out to determine if despair or solitude had a measurable influence on function decline and life span.[2] The mean age of the subjects was seventy-one, and they invited a pool of 1,604 elderly volunteers to respond.

Beginning in 2002, they asked a series of questions to establish a baseline. Participants were asked if they felt left out, if they felt isolated, and finally, if they lacked companionship. More than 43 percent of the participants stated that they often felt lonely or did not engage in companionship activities.

Over the next six years at two-year intervals, scientists evaluated the research participants. They measured time to death as a primary outcome. They also measured changes in stair climbing, mobility, upper-extremity tasks, and general activities of daily living. Those who saw themselves as lonely individuals experienced pronounced decline in daily function and were 8 percent more likely to experience an early demise than their chummy peers.

Dr. Perissinotto's research shines a light on the role sadness and isolation can play in an older person's health, but even being young doesn't mean you're immune. Chronic loneliness appears to lead to high blood pressure, diminished immune response, coronary artery disease, depression, insomnia, and dementia.

Sound bad? We do know that one the greatest advantages of having friends is the contentment and support you feel knowing that they are there to support, encourage, and love you. Friendship makes you happy, and happy people make friends, and they make good friends. People are drawn to those who exude positive emotion. Much of the experimental research is limited by this basic tango: it is unclear whether the beneficial effects of friendship stem from the friendship itself or the happy feelings associated with it.[3]

Happiness has long been confirmed to produce a wide array of physiological and psychological benefits, from lower stress to enhanced mood.[4] Likewise, since research on the subject only began in the 1960s, there has only been a small number of generations that have been studied. But what feels certain from studying existing data is that isolation is powerfully linked to increased incidence of debilitating psychiatric conditions.

The value of friendship can't be overstated, but making friends is sometimes easier said than done. In assisted-living conditions, it can be quite difficult to meet new people and to replace friends who have passed or drifted away. Also, don't think that because you are married or living with others that you are immune to loneliness. Over 60 percent of lonely people in one study were actually married, indicating that loneliness and being alone are two very different things. Finding and nurturing deep friendships is central to your health. What is even more vital is finding friendships with those who are kindred spirits—friends with whom you have shared understanding and perspectives.

Considering those individuals with whom you share the most precious thing in your life—time—is a way to ensure you have a broad perspective and are enriched by the strengths and experiences of others. Mull over these possible approaches.

Surround yourself with a cadre of friends who broaden your horizons, sharpen your intellect, and make you smile. You will find as you are enriched that you are also enriching them—and you are all smiling.

Seize the day! There's no better way to do this than by celebrating the moments of your life, both big and small. For instance, have an indoor picnic by the fire with you partner while the snow falls in December. Celebrate your friend's promotion by toasting her with champagne. If your son is recognized by his teacher for standing up for another student who was being bullied, surprise him by organizing a sleepover with his closest friends.

Don't be insular. Avoid spending time only with like kind. Seek out friends in other professions, of different ages, and those with varying religious beliefs. For example, a friendship that pairs an atheist with a believer can enrich both parties—they may each discover they have shared values and prod each other to see the world from a different vantage point.

James Rohn has elegantly articulated that you are the average of the five people you spend the most time with. Think about this, and think about who are those five people in your life at this moment. Reflecting on this will give you insight and enable you to consider if these individuals reflect your core values.

Being with someone elderly if you are young will give you greater historical perspective and also provide you with a long view of life. There's benefit to the elderly as well. They can enjoy the fresh spirit, curiosity, and vitality of those who are relatively new to the world—and most importantly, children will alleviate the isolation that many seniors experience. Anna Kudak, coauthor of *What Happy Women Do*, said, "Friendships with older and younger people help broaden your perspective, which in turn allows you to have compassion and empathy in your day-to-day life."[5]

Hold those close who have a loving and giving spirit. Negativity can breed negativity whereas those who exude positivity and good cheer can't help but influence all those around them in the best possible way.

"A positive attitude causes a chain reaction of positive thoughts, events, and outcomes. It is a catalyst, and it sparks extraordinary results," as Wade Boggs said.

Remember, optimism and sunny dispositions are contagious.

PRACTICE FORGIVENESS

Darkness cannot drive out darkness; only light can do that. Hate cannot drive out hate; only love can do that.
—MARTIN LUTHER KING JR.

It is important to understand that forgiveness does not erase the past, but it brings solace in the present and can surely bring forth joy in the future. Forgiveness is central to successfully navigating life's troubles. It is fundamental to spiritual growth, and it is absolutely essential to happiness.

If one thing is certain, it's that painful experiences are a part of life. Importantly, forgiveness is the precursor to change and growth, offering a new perspective from which to view you the world. As Rumi wrote, "The wound is the place where the light enters you."

Pain can't be avoided, but how it affects your life in the aftermath of the experience *is* entirely up to you; it's a personal decision. When a person hurts you, whether it's a minor offense or a horrifying calamity, the event itself passes immediately. What remains with you is simply a thought or a feeling—a lingering memory of the hurt.

When your neighbor accidentally cuts down one of your shade trees, the offense itself happens quickly. It is the memory that loiters and is obtrusive. It is the carried grudge that poisons your mind and your neighborhood association meetings and stops you from wanting to see your neighbors in the future.

The offense you experience certainly damages your relationships with those who have offended you, but the lingering pain is the grudge itself that you carry with you and that you nurse by continually or repeatedly revisiting it.

Everett Worthington studies the effects of forgiveness and what he calls *unforgiveness*—the amount of grudge, bitterness, and resentment we hang on to over days, months, or even years. In his experiments, he asks participants to recount a specific personal offense. In these subjects, their blood pressure rises and their heart rates increase. Stress levels rise while the story is being told. Over time, these biological markers of rancor decrease to normal. However, some people return to a normal state much faster than others, indicating that there is a biological predisposition to people's ability to forgive.

Whether because of a unique genetic nervous system structure or due to social upbringing, there are definite psychological and physiological differences in letting go of bitterness and grudges. Worthington mentions that many tend to ruminate upon grievances, trotting them out to repeatedly mull them over occasionally. This practice serves to keep the pain on our minds and in our hearts.

In fact, memory is central to prolonging pain from a slight or tragedy. Beirut is a place that has known excessive war, death, and conquest over the centuries. Archaeological digs uncover layer after layer of history that tells a story of strife and that points to a legacy of grief, dating back from ancient Rome to the crusades and modern-day acts of terrorism. The pain lingering from these tragedies is carried from generation to generation through actions and observations.

To ameliorate this legacy burden of pain in the center of the war-torn city, Alexandra Asseily is overseeing the construction of the Garden of Forgiveness. It is called Solidere, and it will become a place where the people of Lebanon can come and let go of ages of hurt. It is a central site of healing.[6]

Letting go is important to good mental health, and it is the responsibility of the offended person to actively forgive. In the Jewish religion, if a man offends someone, the offender must ask for forgiveness. If he is not forgiven, he must later ask again. If forgiveness is withheld three times, it is then the offended person's responsibility to bear the blame for any remaining rancor. The initial offense may have caused some amount of damage, but it is the lingering, dwelling grudge that causes even more. If a person makes a conscious decision to inflict hurt upon himself by nursing hatred over an offense, the guilt no longer lies with the offender.[7]

Forgiving isn't an easy process. It takes preparation, patience, and more practice. Wayne Dyer championed the field of forgiveness for many decades. He says forgiving yourself is the most important thing, and it can often be instrumental in forgiving others.[8]

Surround yourself with a cadre of friends who broaden your horizons, sharpen your intellect, and make you smile. You will find as you are enriched that you are also enriching them—and you are all smiling.

As an example, you have a favorite apple tree that sparked fond memories of your childhood—and your neighbor cut it down. For as long as you can remember, each summer your father would plant an apple tree. Those summer days were occasions of joy and family connectedness. Unfortunately, one especially beautiful tree—a favorite of yours—began to lean over your neighbor's house. You think he should let it go because he enjoys its beauty, and it also poses no harm, but he sees it differently. He complains frequently and quite vocally until you eventually consent to let him cut it down.

Now you're upset for two reasons—at him for being so persistent and at yourself for not holding your ground. You feel you gave in too easily, whereas you could have held out for many years. Letting go of your guilt isn't easy either, especially with the pleasant memories of your father planting the tree and your swinging from it throughout your youth. You feel like you've let your father down as well. It's also difficult to forgive your neighbor for creating the situation.

So how do you forgive both yourself and him? How do you move on?

The founder of *Tiny Buddha* says you first must forgive yourself and release yourself from the painful story.[9]

It may sound easier said than done. Here are the steps.

1. *Move on.* Remember that the offense is in the past, and it can only affect your happiness if you carry it forward.

2. *Shift your focus from blame to understanding.* Allow the full range of feelings—from pain to understanding to positivity—to permeate you, but do not judge them. Do not judge anyone. Simply feel what you wish to feel. Dyer says, "Shift your mental energy to allowing yourself to be with whatever you're feeling—let the experience be, without blaming others for your feelings."[10]

3. *Avoid telling others what to do or how to react to the incident.* This will make forgiveness less necessary, as people will not offend you with falling short of your expectations. Remember that people are perfectly capable of making their own decisions, and if they offend you, it may be because you have made yourself into an easily offended person.

4. *Be like water.* Do not dominate or try to change the people around you. Try to flow around the stones, bend with the wind, and roll with the punches. Accept that humans are flawed, and we will inevitably hurt each other, even by accident.

5. *Take responsibility for your part in the offense.* This will keep you from further victimizing yourself. If you had a hand in the offense—even minor—forgive yourself. If you truly did not have a hand in the offense, take responsibility for letting it go.

6. *Be kind instead of right.* A Chinese proverb says if you're going to pursue revenge, you'd better dig two graves. In other words, if you choose to carry resentment about something a person has done or said, and if you act on that resentment in any way, you will not be righting the wrong; you will simply double the amount of resentment stemming from the offense. Kindness is an active choice that relegates the hurt to the rearview mirror—it is simply behind both of you.

7. *Think like a social creature.* Remind yourself of how much forgiveness would mean to you if it were you who made the mistake. Putting yourself in the shoes of the person who hurt you can go a long way toward aiding understanding. Did you ever have a fender bender and feel angry because a distracted driver has damaged your car? As a result, you will now have to deal with tedious paperwork and time spent on car repairs. Consider that this individual may have life pressures you know nothing about. Can you find empathy in your heart for this individual? Consider what a precious gift this is for both that person and yourself.

As Rumi wrote, "The wound is the place where the light enters you."

8. *Don't look for occasions to be offended.* If you look for offense, you will always find it. Ever gotten mad at a dog over something? When the dog chews your slipper, it may irritate you, but you don't take it personally. You are likely only offended by a sense of premeditated harm or a personal offense. It is helpful to assume the best of people. Don't assume they are acting out of malice. Often they have personal motivators that are unrelated to you. Most people are not consciously trying to harm others with words and actions, and this is especially true for those you love.

Send love. No matter what, love will always feel better than hate. If you decide to love the person you are harboring a grudge against, it will lighten your own heart and the hearts of those around you. After all, isn't removing the hurt exactly what you want? Who wants to relive the slight over and over? Giving and receiving love is a cleansing process that reduces stress and eliminates resentment. It is difficult to be angry with someone while thinking loving thoughts about them. And you will relieve the pressure on others who are affected by choosing to let go. This is a gift to yourself, the offender, and others who share in the pain.

Forgiveness is for you, not them. It is your life that you are trying to improve with forgiveness. It is your life that will be lightened with love. The weight of rancor is yours alone to carry or you can simply choose to put it down.

But why should you love a person who has wronged you? Here's the most important reason: forgiveness is for you, not them. It is your life that you are trying to improve with forgiveness. It is your life that will be lightened with love. The weight of rancor is yours alone to carry—or you can simply choose to put it down.

Remember, as Thích Nhất Hạnh said, "Compassion is a verb."

LISTEN TO MUSIC

Bob Marley said it best: "One good thing about music, when it hits you, you feel no pain."

Music has been common to all cultures, in every part of the world, throughout all time. There is even some evidence in the form of primitive flutes found in ancient archaeological sites that music may have preceded language. Music is a boon to mood and serves as a tool for productivity, whether we are revving up for a football game, celebrating joy at a wedding, or getting in the zone at the gym.

Imagine a single experience that can lift you up, tear you down, energize you, calm you, anger you, make you weep with joy, put you to sleep, and wake you up. Music does all of this. It is an amazing product of human intelligence, and in it is reflected everything that makes us human: every emotion, every dream, every fear, from our flutist ancient ancestors to our lullaby-listening infants. Music taps into the whole brain and carries with it the power of the whole human experience.

When we listen to music, a variety of effects cascade along the beat of our daily life. Stress is immediately reduced, moods change, work becomes more focused, sleep comes without a fight. What's more exciting is that we can track the benefits of music and apply them to our life at will once we know how. Let's look at several of the benefits of music and how to use them to our best advantage.

Stress Reduction and Relaxation

The potent effect of music is the ability to enable us to instantly relax and de-stress. Researchers at the University of Missouri found that listening to music when angry or depressed provides immediate relief.[11] Low-tempo, mellow music is an obvious choice, but it turns out that if you listen to music you enjoy, it will help no matter what the tempo. Individuals respond differently to different kinds of music, and what sounds aggressive and harsh to one person may sound energizing and empowering to another.

It has also been found that patients who listened to music prior to an operation had lower stress levels than when taking antianxiety medication. Music prevents stress-related increases in heart rate, blood pressure, and cortisol levels prior to surgery. Another study revealed that music helped heart surgery patients to recover with significantly less morphine to manage pain. The study found that music and morphine can do the very same thing.

A Dose of Music

Music's ability to produce calming, euphoric effects is rooted in the biology of the brain. When a person listens to music, the whole brain is engaged. Areas dedicated to language, long-term memory, and short-term memory are stimulated. When we listen to music that we really like or that gives us the chills, the neurochemical dopamine is released.

Music and morphine work the same way because they both introduce this "feel good" neurotransmitter into your brain's striatum. The striatum is an area that responds to rewarding stimuli, like food and sex. This is likely why people list music in the top-five things that are pleasurable.[12]

The effect of music is well documented. It produces a chemical jolt on the brain. That means that since the whole brain is engaged when grooving, real changes can be made to your brain's abilities and general balance. Choosing what music to listen to can impact how you feel. It can relax you for an operation, and it can get you ready for your day.

Focus, Energize, Hit the Zone

Teresa Amabile, a Harvard Business School professor, and an independent researcher named Steven Kramer proposed to *The New York Times* that employees are far more likely to have new ideas on days when they feel happier. Conventional wisdom suggests that pressure enhances performance, but real-time data show that workers perform better when they are happily engaged in what they do.

So are happy workers more productive, more imaginative, and more motivated? With music dumping dopamine in the "chocolate and sex" center of your brain, it seems to follow that music at work is a good idea. But why wait until you get to work?

The commute can be a hard time of the day, whether you struggle in traffic or ride public transit. Studies have indicated that eliminating a long commute can make employees as happy as a $40,000 raise. If a commute is long, then spending that time listening to music will boost happiness to the tune of a few thousand dollars, at least.

Lose Weight, the Musical

It is probably no surprise that music helps with working out and losing weight. Who doesn't grab an iPod or crank up the stereo when it's time to exercise? Research shows that folks who combine music with a good diet and exercise get more out of their efforts than those who only diet and exercise.

This could be because it is just plain easier to exercise with musical accompaniment. Humans get energized when listening to music, particularly up-tempo and peppy music. Beethoven's "Für Elise" is not going to do the job when practicing your powerlifting; however, songs with a rhythm between 120 and

140 beats per minute (BPM) will make you push harder. Think about how a polka or rock and roll gets you moving.

On top of driving you with a bouncing beat, music helps in fitness training by distracting you from the physical pain of the exertion or inspiring you to push yourself as hard as you can to achieve your dreams. Ever heard the *Rocky* training anthem "Gonna Fly Now" in your head while you work out and strive to get Stallone's abs? It works better than you may think. In fact, music can be used to help create *any* mood. Not just the mood for running up stairs.

Mood Management

Using music to your advantage can become a part of your daily life. The benefits to mind and body can be harnessed with some study and thought and a willingness to let tunes change your 'tude. A playlist can be created for every type of mood you wish to boost, from sleepiness to happiness. The place to start is a checklist. The next time you hear a song that gives you that shiver down your spine or an adrenaline rush, take a moment to reflect. In the book *Your Playlist Can Change Your Life: 10 Proven Ways Your Favorite Music Can Revolutionize Your Health, Memory, Organization, Alertness, and More*, the authors make a few suggestions on how to apply music to your life in a practical way. They suggest answering the following questions using a five-star rating system, just like the ones on iTunes and other music media players.

- How **relaxed** does this song make me feel?
- How **happy** does this song make me feel?
- How **energized** does this song make me feel?

- How **motivated** and inspired does this song make me feel?
- How **focused** do I feel when I listen to this song?

When we listen to music a variety of effects cascade along the beat of our daily life. Stress is immediately reduced, moods change, work becomes more focused, sleep comes without a fight. What's more exciting is that we can track the benefits of music and apply them to our life at will, once we know how. Let's look at several of the benefits of music, and how to use them to our best advantage.

Once you have gathered some answers about your own tastes and what drives you toward certain moods, you can assemble playlists for each occasion. Try to make several playlists, for different goals, such as "Rocky champ workout" or "lonely without chocolate at bedtime."

Best Music for the Big Happy

The number-one most-sought-after mood is happiness, so what does the research show regarding music that boosts happiness? This is the most studied emotional impact of music. Jack Lewis, a neuroscientist studying music's effect on happiness, discovered that consonant, upbeat music in a major key is most effective.[13]

Consonance is the quality of notes matching each other. Cultural differences can change what people consider consonant, but if you grew up exposed to Western culture, for example, then fast-paced, predictable melodies in a major key are the choice for you if you want to boost your happiness.

According to research, pop music is a good choice for increasing your happiness quotient, especially if the songs are familiar. Familiar songs give us an extra boost, as the dopamine infusion of happy music combines with feel-good chemicals produced by pleasant memories. We all get a lift out of listening to the same song that played when we first learned to drive or had our first kiss. Music engages the memory sections of the brain quite heavily, so find songs that hit you hard, until you feel no pain.

Lewis compiled a list of Songs by Science. The songs listed below are scientifically proven to make you feel chipper.

- Prince—"Sexy Dancer"
- B. B. King—"Let the Good Times Roll"
- The Beach Boys—"Surfin' USA"
- Curtis Mayfield—"Victory"
- Bob Marley—"Three Little Birds"
- Muddy Waters—"Got My Mojo Workin'"
- Boney M.—"Sunny"
- The Darkness—"I Believe in a Thing Called Love"
- Scissor Sisters—"Take Your Mama"
- OutKast—"Hey Ya!"
- The Futureheads—"Acapella"
- Daft Punk—"Harder, Better, Faster, Stronger"
- M People—"Movin' on Up"
- Tchaikovsky—*1812 Overture*

An entertaining work exercise is to ask your office colleagues what music makes them happy and create a playlist with all of these songs. You will notice the immediate joyful effect it has on your coworkers.

The Mind-Body Connection

To get the most out of musical medicine, there needs to be a certain level of commitment to the idea of grooving or rocking out. The mind must be willing for the body to hear the music.

A study published in *The Journal of Positive Psychology* found that those participants who were given happy music to listen to and instructions to try to feel happier fared better than those who were only given happy music, without instruction.

This attention to one's own mind and body is termed *mindfulness*, and it is the pathway to success in mood management. A strong connection to our emotional core allows music to bring forth what we most desire—joyfulness.

Humans are hardwired for empathy, and our emotions are mirrored in the emotions of other listeners. Lewis discovered this truth as well when he found that acapella music created a strong sense of bonding and happiness. He said, "Music is so ingrained into humans that it doesn't need instruments to have an effect on us. When we hear emotion in a human voice our brains are tuned to feel some of this emotion ourselves."

We react to the emotions in the human voices of the singers whether or not they are accompanied by instruments. In an acapella song, we bond with the artists. Even a song in another language can evoke empathetic responses. "La Llorona" from the movie *Frida* is a song that conveys its emotional gravity whether you speak Spanish or not and whether you see the video or not. Chills abound as an old woman sings a despairing song of a murdering ghost-mother, even if one does not know of the Hispanic urban legend about La Llorona.

Tips to Enhance Your Day with Music

Matching the music to the setting is important for it to be effective. Armed with assorted playlists, any day can be highlighted with golden melodies if properly selected. Check out this list of tips for picking the right anthem for your day.

- Wake up to whatever gives you musical energy. Upbeat music can get you up faster, but gentle and calming music can keep you from worrying about an upcoming stressful meeting.

- ◆ At work, what you listen to depends on what you are doing:
  - If your work involves numbers or attention to detail, listen to classical music.
  - Listen to pop music if your work involves data entry.
  - If your work involves solving equations, listen to ambient music.
  - If you need to problem-solve at work, listen to dance music.[14]
- ◆ At the gym, push the tempo up to 120 BPM or more.
- ◆ Sing along, hum, or just snap your fingers. Playing music hits the right spots too.
- ◆ Bedtime beats should be at around 60 BPM and include some nostalgia.
- ◆ Pick songs you know and like throughout your day. Pleasure centers light up when you get those chills. However, research participants who did not choose the music they were listening to did not get the same pleasure effects and pleasure center stimulation.[15]
- ◆ That said, for overall general pleasure, don't forget the delight of hearing an old song you had forgotten about or a new one that tears your heart out.

Get a Move On!

James Brown was an energetic performer, and the effect of his contagious energy was never more evident than when he yowled, "I feel good!" Ecstatically singing and dancing brought

Mr. Brown health, wealth, and happiness. He sang, "I feel good! I knew that I would!" Get up and move to it and you, too, can *feel good*!

At the Beckman Institute in Illinois, scientists are currently studying the positive impact of movement and energy.[16] Mood is boosted, of course, through the innate opioid release commonly known as "runner's high." But running isn't the only way to move, of course, and runner's high isn't the only benefit of exercise. Vascular health is improved, which means improved circulation to the brain.

When exercising, neurotropic chemicals get squeezed into your system, including brain-derived neurotrophic factor (BDNF), a neuron cell growth stimulator. On top of that, your brain gets better nutrition as glucose and lipid metabolism are cranked up to power your joyous exercise. The brain gets the same boost as your heart, so don't forget to exercise before putting on your thinking cap.

Luckily, vigorous movement gets your brain, as well as your body, in shape. Over time, with exercise, thinking gets easier, just like that uphill section of your daily run challenges the body to get stronger.

In 2014, researchers at the University of Illinois at Urbana–Champaign linked physical activity with increased white matter of the brain.[17] White matter comprises the portion of our brains that carries signals across clusters of cell bodies (gray matter), like superhighways. A strong, tight white matter network means faster processing speeds and excellent memory and retrieval.

Studies show that physical exertion improved these biological structures of the brain, creating denser microfiber arrangements in young and old participants. That's right, jogging can tone your abs and your cerebrum simultaneously.[18]

Why white matter adores exercise is unclear, but one possibility is improved cardiovascular flow. White matter is mainly composed of lipid tissue (fat). Capillaries run through these long, fat-sheathed connections, allowing blood to flow and new vessels and sheaths to be formed. When the blood gets pumping during exercise, the very essence of life courses through your brain.

There are dozens of ways to get some physical exercise each day. Listening to "Physical" by Olivia Newton-John is a good start, in fact. Dance is the happiest form of fitness. There is a reason people go out to dance at clubs when they want to let off steam at the end of the week. Grooving has been a stress reliever for humanity since the days of celebrating mammoth hunts with a victory dance.

A group of Swedish researchers studied 112 teenage girls who struggled with pain, stress, anxiety, and depression. The girls were divided into a dance class group and a control group. Those in the dance class reported a mood boost and better sustained mental health, even up to eight months after the classes ended.[19]

Other researchers at the University of Derby in their own study on the sexy-happy effects of salsa lessons cite the endorphin release from exercise as the cause of these improvements. In addition to the good old runner's high, there is the added element of social interaction, a thing we humans crave.

Learning to dance and feeling confident while dancing, just like learning any new skill, increases self-confidence as well—

something that is essential to everyone, not just teenage girls. Not to be out-boogied by the Swedes or the English, German scientists examined twenty-two tango dancers to see how their stress levels compared to the more lead-footed population.[20] The sultry and complicated footwork gave the participants confidence and significantly lowered depression and cortisol, a stress hormone. Testosterone levels and feelings of sexy, relaxed empowerment were high, which is only to be expected after learning to dance.

Dana Santas is a pro athlete yoga instructor who developed Radius Yoga Conditioning, a style of yoga designed to help athletes move, breathe, and better focus. She has been helping professional sports teams such as the Atlanta Braves and the Orlando Magic to perform to the best of their ability—both on and off the field. To her, confident health is as easy as one, two, three. She has developed a short yoga routine intended to quickly boost happiness, based on three versions of the warrior pose. Holding these poses for just five breaths on each side takes about two minutes altogether, and the impact is felt immediately.

Science has shown that we can efficiently reverse the physiological response to emotional stimuli by consciously altering our postures and thoughts. Just a few minutes of deep breathing will stimulate your parasympathetic nervous system, which is responsible for lowering cortisol, blood pressure, and heart rate. With this in mind, Santas developed an effective yoga routine to spark serenity. Her routine is based on poses, breathing, and meditation.

Diaphragmatic breathing is essential to relaxation. To practice, simply inhale deeply and focus on expanding your lower ribs without arching your back. Then slowly exhale, pushing all the air out from the deepest corners of your lungs. Do this for ninety seconds and you're on your way.

A wonderful side effect of this breathing routine is that it intensifies your awareness of the moment. It is surprisingly difficult to worry about unpaid bills and other daily concerns while concentrating on your breathing. Focus all your attention on the flow of air moving through your nose, throat, and chest. How does it feel when your lungs are filled? Can you expand yourself even more with the next breath? Try relaxing your eyelids while breathing, or feel the gentle breath across your lips as you exhale through your mouth.

This sets the stage for yoga poses that are described below.[21] Warrior is an open-body pose, which a 2010 Harvard study showed was responsible for increasing testosterone, bringing feelings of confidence and self-assuredness, and reducing cortisol, all leading to a stress-free state of power-bliss.

Warrior one

From standing, step back into a lunge but drop your back heel and point your toes out 45 degrees. Keep your back leg straight with your forward knee flexed above your ankle. Lift your arms overhead, shoulder-distance apart. Hold for five long, deep breaths. Repeat on the other side.

Warrior two

Step your right leg back, as though you are coming into a lunge position, but drop the right heel and point the toes out to almost 90 degrees. Keep your right leg straight with your left knee bent to align above your ankle. With your shoulders aligned above your hips, reach your right arm back and left arm forward with your palms down. Look past your front hand and take five long, deep breaths. Repeat on the other side.

Warrior three

Shift your weight into your right leg and begin to take weight off your left leg. Exhale fully to drop your rib cage and have better access to core muscles to help stabilize you. When you feel steady, reach your arms forward and left leg back along a horizontal line. Try to hold it for two or three breaths. Repeat on the other side.

There is also a body of intriguing scientific evidence indicating that couples who sweat together, stay together. Working out together will not only improve the efficiency of your workout but there's this wonderful bonus—it's a way to further your bond.[22] After all, exercising together can make your hearts flutter. The effects of working out—sweating, heavy breathing, flushed skin—are also the hallmarks of physical love and can be used to trigger or strengthen physical attraction to your partner. Of course, the physiological benefits of exercise, like muscle tone and endurance, also add to the desirability quotient in the bedroom.

Since the 1960s, it has been known that just having someone present when you work out will increase your probability of finishing it. However, don't turn your workout buddy into your coach. This may threaten to stress your relationship and hinder progress. It is important to consider that your workout buddy doesn't have to live in the same city. He or she can live hundreds of miles away, and you can plan an exercise routine together and have a daily check-in.

The shared experience is a great source of validation, and if you're a runner, sharing a runner's high is a powerful bonding experience. Jointly exercising also invokes the innate benefits of mimicry and mirroring. Nonverbal matching behaviors create a subconscious bond that can be the foundation of meaningful relationships.[23]

Some tips to get you moving and keep you there include the following:

- *Find an exercise buddy.* Even if you can't make it to the gym together, find someone you can count on to keep you on task. They can live halfway across the country, so long as they are committed to moving to feel good. Tell them your exercise plans and have them check up on you! And you do the same for them.
- *Have your doctor write an exercise prescription.* Refills are infinite. It will get you out of your office or cubicle and maybe even out of the building for a bit. You might want to wave your scrip at the boss as you head for the sunshine.
- *Track your success.* Get a Fitbit or similar wearable device to provide yourself with feedback on your hard work. Sure, rock-hard abs and accelerated thinking are great, but where is the pie chart? Fitbit has an ex-

cellent app that tracks your goals, gives you pats on the back (we all love that!), and tells your friends (see "Find an exercise buddy" above).

◆ *Take a yoga class.* Doing yoga with a friend is terrific, and classes or a regular meet-up can give you all the benefits of an exercise buddy combined with education on self-improvement and social rewards! For an all-around mind-body boost, it is hard to beat yoga with a group of friends.

◆ *Avoid a sedentary lifestyle.* In studies at the Beckman Institute, the quantity or intensity of exercise has been shown to be unimportant to the neurological outcomes. It was simply doing physical activity that was positively correlated with white matter strength. Just get up and move a little each hour. The Fitbit has an alarm for that too. So does your phone.

◆ *Sing in the shower.* Just do it! It makes you feel good. But don't dance. Too slippery.

MEDITATION

Your beliefs become your thoughts,
Your thoughts become your words,
Your words become your actions,
Your actions become your habits,
Your habits become your values,
Your values become your destiny.

—MAHATMA GANDHI

Meditation and Children

Meditation is truly for everyone, regardless of age. The benefits to adults have been well documented, but did you know that children can also reap the tremendous rewards of meditation?

Nothing makes this point as well on one study in particular that used meditation to address issues of attention deficit hyperactivity disorder (ADHD), which has become a common malady in children throughout the world. That represents a whole lot of little guys and girls. When children affected by ADHD learned to practice meditation, they demonstrated fewer symptoms of the disorder and experienced a reduction or elimination of the ADHD medication.

Bess O'Connor of the Chopra Center suggests there are many ways to encourage children to practice mindfulness. More than working to have them mind what *you* say, they can be taught to mind what *they* are saying—and feeling too. The key is to work with your children to help them understand their feelings and behaviors so that they can have the wonderful enlightenment that comes with a regular practice of meditation—they can control their thoughts, which then control behavior.

O'Connor recommends that the best place to begin is—*you be the change.* Kids model their behavior after their parents, and if they see you taking time to calm yourself, it will be a learned behavior for them. Practicing silence and voluntary time-outs are rudimentary forms of meditation. These basic practices bring attention to the absence of motion and lay the groundwork for more advanced self-control. Try playing "the quiet game," which, for all its ridicule in popular cinema, is, in fact, more difficult than its name implies. It has the benefit of also working for adults because being in a state of quiet can be a challenge for many adults. Try it with your children and see that it will clear your mind of your to-do list and calendar.

To encourage your children to begin this practice, consider guided meditation apps and wearable devices to appeal to their enjoyment of bright colors and flashing lights. The animations found on apps combine healthy meditative activities with screen time.

One simple exercise is to ask your children to pretend they are breathing in the scent of a flower and use their exhaled breath to pretend they are blowing out a candle. You will be surprised how quickly this engages them.

Another exercise is to ask your children to gaze into the flame of a candle or at a lava lamp. The fire and the swirling colors will hold his or her attention long enough to make the transition to tranquility.

One other practice is to have your children lie flat and then instruct them to focus on various parts of their bodies, unwinding the muscles one body part at a time. Start with the toes and work up to the top of the head. Give them something to imagine, such as ants marching along or magic dust sprinkled on their limbs, to relax them.

Meditation and You

Now that you understand the benefits of meditation for children, here's how you can begin your own meditative practice. Find the meditation that's right for you. All the wisdom traditions have espoused the benefits of meditation throughout the ages, and they all have myriad benefits.[24] One particular meditation may suit you the best.

You should meditate at least once a day, and if you don't have time to do that, you should meditate twice a day.

1. Buddhist Meditation

Zen meditation, known as *zazen*, is a technique based on the spiritual techniques of ancient Buddhist monks. Peace is achieved by concentrating on breathing or by simply practicing *effortless presence*—the art of just being.[25]

2. Vipassana

Another Buddhist meditation technique, known as Vipassana, traces its roots back to sixth-century India. Vipassana means *to see things as they really are*. It is often referred to as insight meditation. It is practiced through self-observation by focusing on the deep connection between mind and body.

3. Mindfulness

Mindfulness is the art of being aware of the present moment through nonjudgmental observation of your thoughts and feelings, your breath, or bodily sensation. Active practice looks much like Vipassana, from which it takes its origins. However, mindfulness is considered more a philosophy to be continually practiced than a discrete activity to calm oneself.[26]

4. Loving-Kindness

Loving-kindness meditation is a way to increase compassion. It is essentially a method to cultivate love for yourself and others. It increases serenity by decreasing hostility and resentment. The language of loving-kindness involves silently repeating these words:

May I be filled with loving-kindness.
May I be safe from inner and outer dangers.
May I be well in body and mind.
May I be at ease and happy.

The practices involve four steps. First, direct these words to yourself. Second, direct them to a loved one. Third, direct them to someone about whom you are neutral. Fourth, and perhaps most important, direct them toward someone who has hurt you and to whom you are feeling resentful.

5. Transcendental Meditation

Transcendental meditation, or TM, is an ancient technique from India. It is an effortless meditation that is practiced twice daily for fifteen to twenty minutes. It allows your body to settle into a deep state of relaxation while the mind remains alert. TM allows for the powerful release of accumulated stress and returns you to a state of wholeness, wellness, and happiness.

6. Taoist Meditation

Taoist meditation is associated with ancient Chinese philosophy and the religion of Taoism. The practice is designed to create, manipulate, and circulate internal energy. The techniques involve concentration, insight, and visualization. Using silent focus, usually on breathing, a state of clarity and calmness are achieved, leading to intuitive insights.[27]

7. Christian Meditation

Christian prayer is a scientifically proven and highly effective method of meditation. Some regard prayer as slightly different from other forms of medication in that it is directed outward, whereas many forms of meditation are directed inward—however, the outcomes may be similar. Both prayer and meditation fall under the category of contemplative practices. Contemplative prayer is the repetition of chants or thoughts, often using an instrument such as the rosary. It promotes a feeling of calm and focuses the mind, setting the stage for a more powerful connection to God or self. The beads of the rosary are used to count off repetitions. Catholics are not alone in using beads as part of their daily devotions. Prayer beads are also common in Hinduism (Japa Mala beads), Sikhism, Buddhism, and Islam.[28]

8. Guided Meditations

Guided meditation is a technique where a teacher, therapist, or smartphone speaks to you and gently guides you through a relaxing series of visualizations. Some focus on breathing and use imagery, while others focus on the sounds of nature, such as those made by crickets, waves, or the wind. Myriad forms of these guided tours to tranquility can be found everywhere, from psychiatrist offices to your smartphone and Fitbit stores. Also, guided meditations are found on podcasts featuring motivational speakers, therapists, and yogis.[29]

Many of these meditations involve breathing, but all of them have the benefit of slowing your breath and increasing your essential life force. Practicing any form of meditation will ultimately breathe new life into you, rekindle your spirit, and bring you closer to achieving your life purpose.

You may think you don't have time to cram meditation into your busy life, but there is a wise adage for you to ponder: you should meditate at least once a day, and if you don't have time to do that, you should meditate twice a day.

"Things to Do in the Belly of the Whale"
Dan Albergotti

Measure the walls. Count the ribs. Notch the long days.
Look up for blue sky through the spout. Make small fires
with the broken hulls of fishing boats. Practice smoke signals.
Call old friends, and listen for echoes of distant voices.
Organize your calendar. Dream of the beach. Look each way
for the dim glow of light. Work on your reports. Review
each of your life's ten million choices. Endure moments
of self-loathing. Find the evidence of those before you.
Destroy it. Try to be very quiet, and listen for the sound
of gears and moving water. Listen for the sound of your heart.
Be thankful that you are here, swallowed with all hope,
where you can rest and wait. Be nostalgic. Think of all
the things you did and could have done. Remember
treading water in the center of the still night sea, your toes
pointing again and again down, down into the black depths.

7

Seven Simple Steps to a Happier You

Infuse your life with action. Don't wait for it to happen.
Make it happen. Make your own fortune. Make your
own hope. Make your own love. . . . [Do] what you can
to make grace happen.

— BRADLEY WHITFORD

Think of how wonderful it is to know that when others think of you, they say, "My life is better for having known her," or "I can't imagine how rich my life is because he is in it."

This is a benediction. A life that is lived with purpose graces the lives of others. And doesn't it make you happy to know that you make others happier?

By now, you may have learned the secret and the shortcut to happiness. The shortcut is to consciously embrace your life's unique purpose using the tools of self-awareness, service, and kindness.

And by offering you a shortcut, we'll help you avoid the "long cut"—which is looking for happiness in all the wrong places. You don't need to look far, because happiness is lurking all around you. It's right here. But to find it, you must have your eyes and your heart wide open, and only then will you find it in abundance.

One of the most famous experiments in psychology that teaches us about being present is called "the Gorilla in Our Midst."[1] The experiment involved individuals watching a video in which they were asked to count how many times a basketball was passed among players dressed in white. In the midst of the video, as the ball is being passed, a man dressed in a gorilla suit walks across the court. Surprisingly, perhaps, about half of those who viewed the video didn't even notice the gorilla because they were so intent on watching the ball being passed. Later, when told they had missed the gorilla, they were skeptical. How was this possible?

The experiment underscores a key fact that also pertains to happiness—many of us miss much of what occurs directly in front of us. Happiness is right in front of you if you choose to see it. It's there in the flowers that grace your neighbor's yard, in cumulous clouds that stand out in the bluest sky, and a conversation with a coworker that enriches your day. So many of us miss these experiences because we are watching the proverbial ball being passed—or looking at our phones.

So now, look up.

You have before you stories of individuals who have used adversity as a turning point in their lives, people who have suffered loss, been treated unfairly, or witnessed inequity and who have used that experience to do good work and to enrich the lives of others. While often the stories recount transformational changes where hundreds or thousands have benefited from the good work of these remarkable individuals, the benefit is also available to you on a scale both grand or small.

Each of us can influence the lives of others by extending a hand, supporting a charity, and by simply paying attention. The ripple effect of these actions has the potential to resonate for days, months, years, or even generations.

His Holiness the Fourteenth Dalai Lama said, We are visitors on this planet. We are here for ninety or one hundred years at the very most. During that period we must try to do something good, something useful, with our lives. If you contribute to other people's happiness, you will find the true goal, the true meaning of life.[2]

Artfully said, but how do we take the first step?

Following are some suggested and simple acts of kindness that will enrich the lives of others and boomerang much of the good feeling generated right back at you.

- ◆ Pay the toll for the car that follows you through a toll-booth.
- ◆ At Starbucks or Dunkin' Donuts, when you pay for your coffee, leave money to pay for the order of the person behind you—and leave before he or she can thank you.
- ◆ Take the time to ask for the name of your server at a restaurant and write "Thank you," using the person's

name when you leave a tip. Also ask for the name of a grocery checkout clerk and the person who delivers your pizza—and use it.

- Surprise someone by letting them go ahead of you in the grocery line.
- Compliment a colleague for being gracious and responsive, but make sure the compliment is specific and true.
- When exiting an airplane, thank the crew for a safe flight and for all they did to make it comfortable.
- Volunteer at a senior center, food bank, or animal shelter.
- Donate to a charity that advances a cause close to your heart.

These simple acts will radiate goodwill into the lives of others and incentivize them to replicate your kindness. Your goodness is pushed out into the world and will radiate far beyond your good deed. Small, generous acts on your part will contribute to a kinder, gentler world.

But what about days when your own goodwill is taxed by petty or large annoyances?

- When you have waited for twenty minutes to reach a customer service call center and find the representative unhelpful, ask for the person's name and say, "You must be very busy. Thank you for taking time to help me with this."
- When someone cuts you off in traffic and blares the car horn at you, be gracious and wave them forward.

- When you're waiting for service and the person in front of you is painfully slow or disorganized, offer to help.
- When someone cuts you off—in line or in conversation—use it as an opportunity to smile and be patient.

Certainly there will be times in your life when you nurse a grudge over a personal slight that was unexpected and undeserved. Your instinct may be to harbor bad feelings, respond with curtness, or express frustration. But before you do, here is a simple truth that, when fully embraced, will prove life-changing:

> Be kind, for everyone you meet is fighting a battle you know nothing about.

You cannot know if the person who cuts you off in traffic is worried that he may be fired if he's late for work, if the woman at the call center recently received a cancer diagnosis, if a co-worker who is rude is struggling with marital woes or a sick child.

These are things you cannot possibly know, but what you can know with certainty is that each person you encounter will be grateful for your understanding.

And in addition to being kind to others, remember this: it is important to always be kind to yourself. A happy life is one in which you forgive yourself for your shortcomings and are grateful for all that you have. Through your actions, you can plant seeds that lead to future joy for others but begin with compassion for yourself.

His Holiness the Fourteenth Dalai Lama said, "We are visitors on this planet. We are here for ninety or one hundred years at the very most. During that period we must try to do something good, something useful, with our lives. If you contribute to other people's happiness, you will find the true goal, the true meaning of life."

To jump-start your journey to happiness, here are some lists of positive books, exercises, songs, movies, songs, TED Talks, and websites that will serve as catalysts guaranteed to enhance your happiness quotient. Refer to them periodically and use the blank lines to add your own suggestions.

THINGS TO MAKE YOU HAPPY

Seven Books

- *Daily Gratitude: 365 Days of Gratitude*
- *The Alchemist*—Paulo Coelho
- *The Little Prince*—Antoine de Saint-Exupéry
- *Staying Alive: Real Poems for Unreal Times*—Neil Astley
- *Jewels of Remembrance: A Daybook of Spiritual Guidance Containing 365 Selections from the Wisdom of Rumi*—Camille Helminski
- *Gratitude*—Oliver Sacks
- *Peter Pan*—J. M. Barrie

What are your favorites?

_____

_____

_____

Seven Websites

- BrainPickings: https://www.brainpickings.org/
- SuperSoul Sunday: http://www.supersoul.tv/
- The Writer's Almanac—a poem each day: http://writersalmanac.org/
- Wayne Dyer—an internationally renowned author and speaker in the field of self-development: http://www.drwaynedyer.com/
- On Being with Krista Tippett—the big questions of meaning: http://www.onbeing.org

- Heartbeings: https://www.heartbeings.com/
- Everyday Power—a motivational blog that makes positive breaking news: https://everydaypowerblog.com/

What are your favorites?

_____

_____

_____

_____

Seven TED Talks

- Dan Gilbert: "The Surprising Science of Happiness"
  - Dan Gilbert gave his first TED Talk in February 2004; the surprising science of happiness was one of the first ever published, in September 2006. Here, the Harvard psychologist reminisces about the impact of TED, shares some suggestions of useful further reading—and owns up to some mistakes.

- Brené Brown: "The Power of Vulnerability"
  - Brené Brown studies human connection—our ability to empathize, belong, and love. In a poignant, funny talk, she shares a deep insight from her research, one that sent her on a personal quest to know herself as well as to understand humanity.

- B. J. Miller: "What Really Matters at the End of Life"
  - At the end of our lives, what do we most wish for? For many, it's simply comfort, respect, love.

B. J. Miller is a hospice and palliative medicine physician who thinks deeply about how to create a dignified, graceful end of life for his patients.

◆ David Steindl-Rast: "Want to Be Happy? Be Grateful"
 – The one thing all humans have in common is that each of us wants to be happy, says Brother David Steindl-Rast, a monk and interfaith scholar. And happiness, he suggests, is born from gratitude. An inspiring lesson in slowing down, looking where you're going, and above all, being grateful.

◆ Nancy Etcoff: "Happiness and Its Surprises"
 – Cognitive researcher Nancy Etcoff looks at happiness—the ways we try to achieve and increase it, the way it's untethered to our real circumstances, and its surprising effect on our bodies.

◆ Robert Waldinger: "What Makes a Good Life?"
 – What keeps us happy and healthy as we go through life? If you think it's fame and money, you're not alone—but, according to psychiatrist Robert Waldinger, you're mistaken. As the director of a seventy-five-year-old study on adult development, Waldinger has unprecedented access to data on true happiness and satisfaction.

◆ Matthieu Ricard: "The Habits of Happiness"
 – What is happiness, and how can we all get some? Buddhist monk, photographer, and author Matthieu

Ricard has devoted his life to these questions, and his answer is influenced by his faith as well as by his scientific turn of mind: we can train our minds in habits of happiness.

What are your favorites?

_____

_____

_____

_____

Seven Movies
- *Slumdog Millionaire* (2008)
- *When Harry Met Sally* (1989)
- *Love Actually* (2003)
- *Roman Holiday* (1953)
- *Cinema Paradiso* (1988)
- *The Sound of Music* (1965)
- *The Wizard of Oz* (1939)

What are your favorites?

_____

_____

_____

_____

Seven Songs
- "Hallelujah"—Bon Jovi
- "Across the Universe"—The Beatles

- "What a Wonderful World"—Louis Armstrong
- "Con te Partiro"—Sarah Brightman and Andrea Bocelli
- "My Happiness"—Ella Fitzgerald
- "Brindisi" from *La Traviata*—Pavarotti
- "Ode to Joy" from Beethoven's Symphony no. 9 in D Minor, op. 125.

What are your favorites?

_____

_____

_____

_____

Seven Happy Exercises

Here are simple exercises to set you on a path to embracing your own unique life purpose and ensuring that you flourish.

Seven Happiness Apps

- Get Journal—Happy Tapper: The easiest and most effective way to rewire your brain in just five minutes a day, unleashing everything great in you.
- Sing! Karaoke by Smule: Join in the fun. Sing your favorite top hits with artists like Jessie J, Jason Derulo, and Charlie Puth. Create solo, duet, and group videos with singers around the world.
- Simply Yoga by Daily Workout Apps: Your own personal yoga instructor wherever you are.

- Poetry from the Poetry Foundation: With the Poetry Foundation's universal iOS app, you can now take thousands of poems by classic and contemporary poets with you wherever you go.

- Inspire Me Quotes by Happy Planet Apps: Inspire Me Quotes is your virtual inspiration generator for a happier and more meaningful life. Flick through quote pages that have been lovingly handcrafted with timeless words of wisdom from some of the world's greatest minds.

- Track Your Happiness by Matt Killingsworth: Track Your Happiness is a scientific research project that investigates what makes life worth living.

- A Year of Kindness Acts by LanziVision: "Want to be happy? Make someone's day." This is our invitation to you to have some fun while creating a lot of unexpected delight and joy for yourself and for the folks around you by offering you 365 days of kindness—a new idea each day of the year, of ways to express kindness through small, easy-to-do acts.

1. Gratitude Exercises

Gratitude Journal

There are many ways to be attentive to all the good in your life—keeping a journal is just one. Research has shown that keeping a gratitude journal correlates with peace of mind and elevated levels of happiness.

Each night, write in a journal one to three things you are

especially grateful for. Examples might range from the professional to the personal, from the minutiae to the grand:

- I am grateful that I was praised today for leading a discussion in a meeting that helped my colleagues, and I came to a good conclusion over a difficult problem with one of our goals.
- I am grateful that I resolved a conflict with my friend Annette and that we both ended our discussion with a hug and an agreement to have dinner soon.
- I am grateful for the cardinals in my backyard, because they remind me of my mother and how much she loved them.
- I am grateful that my family is healthy and safe, that right now they are all home and asleep in their beds.

Here's a bonus idea: If you express gratitude in your journal for friends or colleagues, why not write to the person and tell him or her? You will feel good about both recognizing the good deed and for passing on the appreciation—and the other person will smile and feel good at having been recognized by you.

Gratitude to Go

Every morning, begin your day by writing down three things you are grateful for. Fold up the piece of paper and carry it with you in your handbag or pocket. For instance:

- There are daffodils blooming in the yard.
- I prepared well and am ready to nail the meeting this morning.
- My daughter got an A on a very difficult test.

Gratitude Shared with a Friend

Find a friend who is going through a difficult time or a friend who would enjoy this exercise. Agree to send each other every day an email that outlines three things you are grateful for. The shared experience will be bonding and thoroughly enjoyable.

"I Love You" Gratitude

Rekindle your marriage or relationship with a daily gratitude. Agree to tell your partner in writing one thing that you love about him or her over a thirty-day period. It can be simple or detailed, serious or fun:

- I am grateful that you chose to live your one life with me.
- I am grateful that you know how to use a hammer.
- I am grateful that over the past twenty years, we have grown closer through adversity and that when our children were challenging us as teenagers, it created a bond between us—and that throughout the years, we never hesitated to support each other.
- I love that you love to buy me beautiful lingerie and that I love to wear it.

2. Thorns, Buds, and Roses

Practice this exercise with your children to inspire an understanding of the complexity of life and to teach them that challenges are often counterbalanced with opportunity.

Around the dinner table or before bed, ask your children to share an experience that frustrated them. Follow up by asking them to identify an opportunity that may have remedied the negative experience. Conclude by asking them what positive may have resulted.

For instance:

> **Thorn:** Some kids on the playground excluded me from a game today. They wouldn't let me join in.
>
> **Bud:** I saw some other kids who were playing in another part of the playground and realized they weren't included either. I decided to go over and talk with them.
>
> **Rose:** I made a new friend because one of these other kids saw me, realized I was sad, and asked me to join them. I got invited for a playdate, and I even got invited to a birthday party. My mother was so happy at how I handled this situation.

Thorns, buds, and roses also works for adults. Try it yourself:

> **Thorn:** I was so disappointed that I had a dinner planned with a friend I hadn't seen in many years, but

he missed his connection in Chicago and was delayed an entire day.

Bud: We both rearranged our schedules to meet tomorrow before our respective dinner meetings.

Rose: We saw each other, and despite the initial disappointment, we had an enjoyable evening. Perhaps I even appreciated our visit more when I realized how much I wanted to see him after he'd missed his flight.

3. Nightly Affirmations

Each night before going to sleep, say an affirmation that will program your brain for happiness. Here are two suggestions—but feel free to build in whatever language will help you achieve your personal ambitions.

> I live with abundance, love, and compassion.
> I will flourish in all that I do and inspire others to do the same.

4. Say Thank You Out Loud to Others

Say thank you to the security officer at work, to the young person who packs your groceries, to your children, to your partner.

Consider saying thank you instead of apologizing. If you keep someone waiting, rather than say "I am sorry I'm late," say "Thank you for being patient with me."

5. Praise Your Colleagues

Write notes to your colleagues to bring them joy and enhance their sense of appreciation. If someone helps you figure out a computer glitch, if someone gives a powerful presentation, if someone offers you a good idea, jot that colleague a quick note to let him or her know the kindness was noticed and appreciated.

6. Ask Your Friends to Relive Their Happy Memories (and Yours Too)

Spend time reliving happy memories with your family and friends. Recall a funny vacation story, a long talk late into the night, or an excursion to a consignment shop with your girlfriends that resulted in beautiful finds. This is a direct route to both smiles and happiness.

7. Find Your Purpose in Thirty Days

For thirty consecutive days, jot down on a three-by-five card three or four things that you did that day. Give each activity a rating from one to ten, equating one with something that made you feel miserable and ten with something that made you feel joyful.

At the end of the month, identify all activities that you rated seven or above. Reflect on these activities. It is likely that you will be able to identify those actions that most resonate and give your life meaning. In these activities, you will find bread crumbs to lead you on a path to a purpose-filled life.

YOUR WORKSHEET

Now to launch your journey, think about all you have learned and complete these exercises.

Begin by writing your life purpose here. Make sure you sign and date it to confirm your commitment.

My purpose in life:

_____

_____

_____

Signature _____

Date _____

What three things can you do *today* to begin achieving your purpose?

_____

_____

_____

What three things can you can do *this year* to advance your life purpose?

_____

_____

_____

What three memories made you feel _____?
  a. Happy

_____

_____

_____

b. Joyful

_____

_____

c. Blissful

_____

_____

_____

Who are the five people you can spend time with who make your life better?

_____ Ed Dan Rick _____

_____

_____

_____

_____

Ask yourself: Are you spending your time with these five people? If not, why?

_____ I found out _____

_____

_____

Recount a random act of kindness that you initiated.

_____

_____

_____

Recount a random act of kindness that someone did for you.

_____

_____

_____

Reflect on how it made you feel. Reflect on how it made the recipient feel.

You initiated _____

Someone else initiated _____

Surprise someone by writing a heartfelt note of gratitude today. (Maybe you can write one short note every day.)

_____

_____

_____

Which charity or worthy cause would most benefit from your support, volunteering, or a monetary contribution?

_____

_____

Finally, and most importantly:

The two most important days of your life:
    a. The day you were born _____
    b. The day you figured out why _____

As you go forward . . . .

    Be grateful.

    Be forgiving.

    Be happy.

    Flourish for all the days of your life.

"The Source of Joy"
Rumi

No one knows what makes the soul wake up
so happy! Maybe a dawn breeze
has blown the veil from the face of God.

A thousand new moons appear.
Roses open laughing.
Hearts become perfect rubies
like those from Badakshan.

The body turns entirely spirit.
Leaves become branches in this wind.

Why is it now so easy to surrender,
even for those already surrendered?

There's no answer to any of this.
No one knows the source of joy.

A poet breathes into a reed flute,
and the tip of every hair makes music.

Shams sails down clods of dirt from the roof,
and we take jobs as doorkeepers for him.

From *The Book of Love*,
translated by Coleman Barks

Our Life Purpose

Collected here to jump-start your own quest is a potpourri of reflections by both of us and a cadre of family and friends. If you have articulated your life purpose, please add it to these and let us hear from you. (2mostimportantdays.com)

Sanjiv
To fulfill my dharma to teach medicine, leadership, and happiness and to do this grounded in humility and with an ardent desire to learn every single day. To treasure with gratitude my family, friends, colleagues, and students who inspire me in countless ways, and, in some small measure, to inspire everyone that I encounter during this amazing life journey.

Gina
To pay attention to this precious world in which we live for such a brief time, to use the light that is our life to radiate kindness, to learn and to use that knowledge to illuminate the darkness, to appreciate, to forgive, and to be grateful.

To serve others, to connect with others, to love and bolster my friends and family, and to enjoy as many moments as I can on this beautiful planet.

◆

My purpose is to have unbridled love for my family. To practice meditation and move toward enlightenment and to share the gift of meditation with others. To enrich my life with music and to live with abundance, success, love, and happiness and make it a rich and fulfilling journey.

◆

My purpose is to access my spiritual depth and resourcefulness to connect with and inspire the world through my example and teachings to live consciously and abundantly, knowing all the while we are not in competition.

◆

To live life to its fullest while giving more than I receive in all walks of life.

◆

I seek to be the best mother and grandmother to my children and grandchildren and to tend my garden with love.

◆

To find people with whom I share a genuine and deep interpersonal connection and to treat them with the utmost respect and dignity. Being an active participant in someone's life will bring him or her serenity through the comfort of knowing that I'm there for that person as a pillar of support and solace during times of strife. People long for the satisfaction that comes from interpersonal relationships because they offer an endlessly renewable source of happiness. The magnitude of this gift will lead to eternal happiness.

◆

My purpose in life is to have exuberant compassion and love for not only my family and friends but also those less fortunate and in dire need.

◆

To participate with individuals and organizations in creating a critical mass for a peaceful, just, sustainable, and healthy world through scientifically and experientially exploring nondual consciousness as the ground of existence and applying this understanding in the enhancement of health, business, leadership, and conflict resolution.

◆

I have not yet found my purpose, but until I do, I will continue to find happiness by being the best friend, daughter, and sister I can be and by being a compassionate caretaker of the animals in my life.

◆

My purpose flows like the water and changes as I change, but I remain steadfast in the prayer that I can fulfill the greatest commandment in small acts of kindness, love, forgiveness, and gratitude, remembering that I am not alone, and as my journey moves forward, I pray that I can give small blessings more than receive.

◆

I desire to leave evidence of being a creative, insightful, dedicated, and resilient scientist, father, and partner and to further advances in health care for those affected by poverty-related infectious diseases. I aspire to teach a new generation of public health clinicians. I strive to be generous, helpful, emotionally available, and to shine a piercing light of understanding on my imperfections. Oh, and I dream of formulating the perfect dirty martini.

◆

I will serve others by my actions and example, as a family physician and teacher, with the goal of expanding happiness. I will look to the edges of what is, to see beyond and innovate. I will repeatedly strive to be grateful for all I have been given, to develop compassion for myself and others, and recognize every day is a gift and adventure to be savored.

◆

My purpose in life is to serve and energize others. It is with profound gratitude that I recognize how privileged I have been to be able to do this.

◆

When I was young, I had not one but several scrapes with death. I began to think perhaps I had some great contribution to the world that compelled the universe to perpetually pluck me from the bosom of death. I kept waiting for my big contribution to arrive. While waiting, I inadvertently raised three incredible children. It began to dawn on me that my benefaction might be my children. Knowing I've done my part, I now look three times before crossing a street.

◆

To love, play, and find joy wherever and whenever possible.

◆

Create and connect to add meaning and make a difference.

◆

My life's purpose is to inspire others to reclaim their lives after trauma. My purpose is to send a message of healing, hope, and possibility through my life of having overcome the devastating effects of paralytic polio and childhood violence.

◆

To touch others' lives, especially those of the people I love, through laughter, compassion, and ideas.

"So Much Happiness"
Naomi Shihab Nye

It is difficult to know what to do with so much happiness.
With sadness there is something to rub against,
a wound to tend with lotion and cloth.
When the world falls in around you, you have pieces to pick up,
something to hold in your hands, like ticket stubs or change.
But happiness floats.
It doesn't need you to hold it down.
It doesn't need anything.
Happiness lands on the roof of the next house, singing,
and disappears when it wants to.
You are happy either way.
Even the fact that you once lived in a peaceful tree house
and now live over a quarry of noise and dust
cannot make you unhappy.
Everything has a life of its own,
it too could wake up filled with possibilities
of coffee cake and ripe peaches,
and love even the floor which needs to be swept,
the soiled linens and scratched records . . .
Since there is no place large enough
to contain so much happiness,
you shrug, you raise your hands, and it flows out of you
into everything you touch. You are not responsible.
You take no credit, as the night sky takes no credit
for the moon, but continues to hold it, and share it,
and in that way, be known.

EPILOGUE

Yesterday, I was clever so I wanted to change the world.
Today, I am wise, so I am changing myself.

—RUMI

We embarked on this journey of exploration and discovery to unearth and share with you the time-honored reflections of both ancient thinkers and modern-day scientists. What would these early philosophers think if they knew that the insights they gleaned would one day be amplified by scientific data? What do these scientists and philosophers teach us about the value of living a life of purpose?

This has been a grand adventure for both of us. It was a happy surprise that this journey also opened new doors and windows in our own lives. What we discovered has both informed and inspired us in so many ways.

Because of this book, our knowledge and our friendship have been greatly enriched.

And now with the door ajar and our hand on the knob, this book comes to an end. But before it swings shut, we leave you with one last story. It is our hope that it will further inform and inspire you.

In 1953, Sir Edmund Hillary and Tenzing Norgay were the first to summit the world's highest mountain—Mount Everest at 29,029 feet—to international acclaim. They earned a spot in history books for all perpetuity.

One would think Sir Hillary would forever consider this his greatest achievement, right?

Not so. At the conclusion of that historic expedition, he returned to base camp, not thinking about himself and all he had achieved. Rather, he turned to the Sherpas and asked, "What can I do for you?"

They responded that Nepal was in dire need of schools and medical clinics.

What resulted from this exchange was a lifetime of service, in which Sir Hillary, a New Zealander, vastly improved the lives of the poor people of Nepal.

When later asked to name the crowning achievement of his life, Sir Hillary responded, "I don't know if I particularly want to be remembered for anything. I have enjoyed great satisfaction from my climb of Everest and my trips to the poles. But there's no doubt, either, that my most worthwhile things have been the building of schools and medical clinics. That has given me more satisfaction than a footprint on a mountain."[1]

As we consider our own life purpose, we may be daunted by stories of such heroic individuals. But our own life purpose doesn't need to be grand or epic. Rather, it can be found in simple acts . . . being kind, being attentive, and being grateful. Really, all you need to do to live a life of purpose is make a meaningful difference in one single person's life.

What is your life purpose?

If you are still on your quest for purpose, we hope this book brings you closer to defining and living it.

At life's end, all of us want to look in the rearview mirror and feel our lives have had meaning and purpose. Oliver Wendell Holmes Jr. said, "Most of us go to our graves with our music still inside us, unplayed."

So right now, let's all take a pledge to play the music that we have inside of us. Let's promise each other that we will dance and sing, in the sunshine and in the rain.

We invite you to share with us your life purpose and any stories or reflections that have led you to it.

Thank you for being a part of this extraordinary journey.

Namaste. Sikhona.

Sanjiv and Gina
(2mostimportantdays.com)

"Ode to Solomon"
Translation by Deepak Chopra

My heart was split,
and a flower appeared;
and grace sprang up;
and it bore fruit for my God.

You split me,
tore my heart open,
filled me with love.

You poured your spirit into me;
I knew you as I know my self.
Speaking waters touched me from your fountain,
the source of life . . .

I swallowed them and was drunk
with the water that never dies.
And my drunkenness was insight,
intimacy with your spirit.

And you have made all things new;
you have showed me all things shining.

You have granted me perfect ease;
I have become like Paradise,

a garden whose fruit is joy;
and you are the sun upon me.

My eyes are radiant with your spirit;
my nostrils fill with your fragrance.
My ears delight in your music,
and my face is covered with your dew . . .

Blessed are the men and women
who are planted in your earth, in your garden,
who grow as your trees and flowers grow,
who transform their darkness into light.

Their roots plunge into darkness;
their faces turn toward light.

All those who love you are beautiful;
they overflow with your presence
so that they can do nothing but good.

There is infinite space in your garden;
all men, all women welcome here;
all they need do is enter.

NOTES

Introduction

1. Julia Kasdorf, "What I Learned from My Mother," Poetry Foundation, https://www.poetryfoundation.org/poems-and-poets/poems/detail/48491.

Chapter 1: What Does It Mean to Live with Purpose?

1. Robert Holden, "I See You! Are You Looking at Me?," Heal Your Life, July 26, 2011, http://www.healyourlife.com/i-see-you%20.
2. Shawna Turner, "Namaste: What It Means and Why We Say It," Elephant Journal, August 14, 2012, http://www.elephantjournal.com/2012/08/namaste-what-it-means-why-we-say-it.
3. Hapacus Team, "The Happiness Formula: $H = S + C + V$," Hapacus, March 11, 2010, http://hapacus.com/blog/the-happiness-formula-h-s-c-v/.
4. Robert Emmons, *Thanks* (New York: Houghton Mifflin, 2007).
5. Kristen Stewart, "The Health Benefits of Saying Thanks," Everyday Health, October 19, 2010, http://www.everydayhealth.com/saying-thanks/the-health-benefits-of-saying-thanks.aspx.
6. J. K. Rowling, "Text of J.K. Rowling's Speech," *Harvard Gazette*, June 5, 2008, http://news.harvard.edu/gazette/story/2008/06/text-of-j-k-rowling-speech.
7. Ibid.
8. Norman Rosenthal, "The Gift of Adversity," Norman Rosenthal's website, https://www.normanrosenthal.com/blog/book/gift-adversity/.

9. Bud Bilanich, "Failure Is Good—As Long as You Learn from It," Bud Bilanich's website, http://www.budbilanich.com/failure-is -good/.

Chapter 2: Who Is Happy?

1. Thomas C. Corley, "Rich Habits Study—Background on Methodology," Rich Habits, June 17, 2016, http://richhabits.net/rich -habits-study-background-on-methodology/.
2. Ethan Dunwill, "What Makes Jewish People So Happy?," *The Times of Israel*, http://blogs.timesofisrael.com/what-makes-jewish-people -so-happy/
3. http://content.time.com/time/business/article/0,8599, 1913256,00.html
4. Alyson Shontell, "This Is What the Happiest Person on Earth Looks Like," *Business Insider*, March 8, 2011, http://www.busi nessinsider.com/this-is-what-the-happiest-person-on-earth -looks-like-2011-3#.
5. Narayan Ammachchi, "Looking for Happiness? You'll Find It Living Closer to the Equator," Nearshore Americas, December 7, 2012, http://www.nearshoreamericas.com/living-closer-equator -happiness/.
6. James Bargent, "Here's What We Can Learn from Colombia— the Happiest Nation in the World," *Washington Post*, January 1, 2016, https://www.washingtonpost.com/news/inspired-life/wp /2016/01/15/heres-what-we-can-learn-from-colombia-the -happiest-nation-in-the-world/.
7. Josh Hrala, "The World Happiness Index 2016 Just Ranked the Happiest Countries on Earth," Science Alert, March 17, 2016, http://www.sciencealert.com/the-world-happiness-index-2016 -just-ranked-the-happiest-countries-on-earth.
8. Visit Denmark, "Happiest People in the World," http://www .visitdenmark.co.uk/en-gb/denmark/art/happiest-people-world.

9. Visit Denmark, "The Art of Danish Hygge," http://www.visit denmark.co.uk/en-gb/denmark/culture/art-danish-hygge.

10. Chloe Pantazi, "The 19 Unhappiest Countries in the World," *Business Insider*, March 17, 2016, http://www.businessinsider.com /the-unhappiest-countries-in-the-world-2016-3.

11. Jessica Migala, "4 Habits the World's Happiest People Have in Common," Health, March 18, 2016, http://news.health.com /2016/03/18/4-habits-the-worlds-happiest-people-have-in -common/.

12. Learning English, "What Is the Relationship Between Age and Happiness?," May 29, 2012, http://learningenglish.voanews.com /a/age-happiness-study/1120961.html.

13. Genevieve Shaw Brown, "Seattle Preschool in a Nursing Home 'Transforms' Elderly Residents," ABC News, June 16, 2015, http:// abcnews.go.com/Lifestyle/seattle-preschool-nursing-home -transforms-elderly-residents/story?id=31803817.

14. Jean Twenge, "Young People Are Happier Than They Used to Be," *Atlantic*, November 5, 2015, http://www.theatlantic.com/health /archive/2015/11/the-age-happiness-connection-is-breaking -down/414349/.

15. Chris Barker and Brian Martin, "Participation: The Happiness Connection," *Journal of Public Deliberation* 7, no. 1 (October 2011), http://www.publicdeliberation.net/cgi/viewcontent.cgi?article =1167&context=jpd.

16. Allen R. McConnell, Christina M. Brown, Tonya M. Shoda, Laura E. Stayton, Colleen E. Martin, "Friends with Benefits: On the Positive Consequences of Pet Ownership," *Journal of Personality and Social Psychology* 101, no. 6 (2011): 1239–1252.

17. Sarah Griffiths, "Why Dogs Really ARE Better Than Cats: Canine Owners Are 'Happier and More Outgoing' Than People with Felines," *Daily Mail*, February 2, 2016, http://www.dailymail.co .uk/sciencetech/article-3426173/Why-dogs-really-better-cats -Canine-owners-happier-outgoing-people-felines.html.

18. HelpGuide.org, "The Health Benefits of Pets," http://www.help guide.org/articles/emotional-health/the-health-benefits-of-pets .htm, content discontinued.

19. Cliff Zukin and Mark Szeltner, *Talent Report: What Workers Want in 2012* (New Brunswick, NJ: John J. Heldrich Center for Workforce Development, 2012), https://www.netimpact.org/sites /default/files/documents/what-workers-want-2012.pdf.

20. Melissa Dahl, "A Classic Psychology Study on Why Winning the Lottery Won't Make You Happier," *New York*, January 13, 2016, http://nymag.com/scienceofus/2016/01/classic-study-on -happiness-and-the-lottery.html.

21. Daniel Kahneman, Alan B. Krueger, David Schkade, Norbert Schwarz, and Arthur A. Stone, "Would You Be Happier If You Were Richer?" (working paper, Princeton University Center for Economic Policy Studies, May 2006, Princeton, NJ), https://web .archive.org/web/20140817103658/http://www.princeton.edu /ceps/workingpapers/125krueger.pdf.

22. 8000 Hours, "Everything You Need to Know about Whether Money Makes You Happy," March 2016, https://80000hours.org /articles/money-and-happiness/.

23. Jay Cassano, "The Science of Why You Should Spent Your Money of Experiences, Not Things," *Fast Company*, March 30, 2015, https://www.fastcoexist.com/3043858/world-changing-ideas /the-science-of-why-you-should-spend-your-money-on -experiences-not-thing.

24. Ellie Krupnick, "Shopping to Be Happy? Study Finds It Can Actually Reduce Sadness," *Huffington Post*, January 28, 2014, http:// www.huffingtonpost.com/2014/01/28/shopping-make-you -happy_n_4679516.html.

25. Kit Yarrow, "Why 'Retail Therapy' Works," *Psychology Today*, May 2, 2013, https://www.psychologytoday.com/blog/the-why -behind-the-buy/201305/why-retail-therapy-works.

26. "Research Suggests Giving Boosts Happiness and May Improve

Health," *Chronicle of Philanthropy*, September 8, 2015, https://www.philanthropy.com/article/Research-Suggests-Giving/232905.

27. Brady Josephson, "Want to Be Happier? Give More. Give Better," *Huffington Post*, January 21, 2015, http://www.huffingtonpost.com/brady-josephson/want-to-be-happier-give-m_b_6175358.html.

28. Nancy Etcoff, *Survival of the Prettiest* (New York: Doubleday, 1999), https://www.nytimes.com/books/first/e/etcoff-prettiest.html.

29. PR Newswire, "MarketResearch.com: The US Beauty and Cosmetics Market Expected to Exceed $62 Billion in 2016," January 26, 2016, http://www.prnewswire.com/news-releases/market researchcom-the-us-beauty-and-cosmetics-market-expected-to-exceed-62-billion-in-2016-300209081.html.

30. Angus Deatona and Raksha Arorab, "Life at the Top: The Benefits of Height," *Economics & Human Biology* 7, no. 2 (July 2009): 133–136, http://www.sciencedirect.com/science/article/pii/S1570677X0900046X.

31. Nabanita Datta Gupta, Nancy L. Etcoff, and Mads M. Jaeger, "Beauty in Mind: The Effects of Physical Attractiveness on Psychological Well-Being and Distress," *Journal of Happiness Studies* 17, no. 3 (June 2016): 1313–1325, http://link.springer.com/article/10.1007/s10902-015-9644-6.

32. http://www.cell.com/neuron/abstract/S0896-6273(01)00491-?_returnURL=http%3A%2F%2Flinkinghub.elsevier.com%2Fretrieve%2Fpii%2FS0896627301004913%3Fshowall%3Dtrue

33. Hrala, "The World Happiness Index 2016."

34. Cynthia Bowers, "Who's Happier, Women or Men?," CBS News, July 30, 2008, http://www.cbsnews.com/news/whos-happier-women-or-men/.

35. Peggy Drexler, "Men, Women and the Pursuit of Happiness," *Huffington Post*, May 26, 2011, http://www.huffingtonpost.com/peggy-drexler/men-women-and-the-pursuit_b_867415.html.

36. Peggy Drexler, "Men, Women, and the Pursuit of Happiness," *Psychology Today*, January 23, 2012, https://www.psychologytoday.com/blog/our-gender-ourselves/201201/men-women-and-the-pursuit-happiness.

37. Anna Petherick, "Gains in Women's Rights Haven't Made Women Happier. Why Is That?," *Guardian*, May 18, 2016, https://www.theguardian.com/lifeandstyle/2016/may/18/womens-rights-happiness-well-being-gender-gap.

38. Deni Kirkova, "Sorry Guys! Women Are Happier Than Men—but They Just Won't Admit It . . . ," *Daily Mail*, October 4, 2013, http://www.dailymail.co.uk/femail/article-2443614/Sorry-guys-Women-happier-men—just-wont-admit-.html.

39. Therese J. Borchard, "This Emotional Life: Why Does Religion Make People Happier?," PsychCentral, January 6, 2010, http://psychcentral.com/blog/archives/2010/01/06/this-emotional-life-why-does-religion-make-people-happier/.

40. Jennifer Dunning, "Religious Believers More Depressed Than Atheists: Study," CBC News, September 20, 2013, http://www.cbc.ca/newsblogs/yourcommunity/2013/09/religious-believers-more-depressed-than-atheists-study.html.

41. Catherine Rampell, "The Happiest Man in America, Annotate," *New York Times*, March 7, 2011, http://economix.blogs.nytimes.com/2011/03/07/the-happiest-man-in-america-annotated/?smid=tw-nytimeseconomix&seid=auto&_r=0.

42. Epiphenom, "Religion, Self Esteem and Psychological Adjustment," Patheos, February 23, 2012, http://www.patheos.com/blogs/epiphenom/2012/02/religion-self-esteem-and-psychological.html.

43. Nigel Barber, "Are Religious People Happier?," *Psychology Today*, November 20, 2012, https://www.psychologytoday.com/blog/the-human-beast/201211/are-religious-people-happier.

44. Trade School, Colleges and Universities, "29 Jobs That Make You Happy and Why They Do," May 2, 2017, http://www.trade-schools.net/articles/jobs-that-make-you-happy.asp.

45. Career Bliss Team, "CareerBliss Happiest Jobs in America—2016," March 7, 2016, https://www.careerbliss.com/facts-and-figures/careerbliss-happiest-and-unhappiest-jobs-in-america-2016/.

46. Chad Brooks, "Teachers & Doctors Happiest at Work," *Business News Daily*, March 28, 2013, http://www.businessnewsdaily.com/4238-teachers-happiest-workers.html.

47. Douglas Quenqua, "Lawyers with Lowest Pay Report More Happiness," *New York Times*, May 12, 2015, http://well.blogs.nytimes.com/2015/05/12/lawyers-with-lowest-pay-report-more-happiness/.

48. Nataly Kogan, "5 Scientifically Proven Ways to Be Happier at Work," *Time*, November 17, 2014, http://time.com/3589837/5-scientifically-proven-ways-to-be-happier-at-w.

Chapter 3: The Scientific Underpinnings

1. M. E. P. Seligman, *Flourish: A Visionary New Understanding of Happiness and Well-Being* (New York: Atria, 2012).

2. TED, "Martin Seligman: The New Era of Positive Psychology," February 2004, https://www.ted.com/talks/martin_seligman_on_the_state_of_psychology.

3. T. Panova and A. Lleras, "Avoidance or Boredom: Negative Mental Health Outcomes Associated with Use of Information and Communication Technologies Depend on Users' Motivations," *Computers in Human Behavior* 58 (2016): 249–258.

4. E. C. Tandoc Jr., P. Ferruccib, and M. Duffy, "Facebook Use, Envy, and Depression Among College Students: Is Facebooking Depressing?," *Computers in Human Behavior* 43 (2015): 139–146.

5. R. F. Baumeister, K. D. Vohs, J. L. Aaker, and E. N. Garbinsky, "Some Key Differences between a Happy Life and a Meaningful Life," *Journal of Positive Psychology* 8, no. 6 (2013): 505–516.

6. Bob Condor, "Purpose in Life = Happiness," *Chicago Tribune*, December 6, 2009, http://www.chicagotribune.com/sns-health-life-purpose-happiness-story.html.

7. R. J. Leider, *The Power of Purpose: Creating Meaning in Your Life and Work*, 3rd ed. (Oakland, CA: Barrett Koehler Publishers, 2015).

8. Chopra Foundation, "Gratitude Study," http://www.choprafoun dation.org/education-research/past-studies/gratitude-study/. We have consolidated Wayne Dyer's 15 Steps into Nine Steps.

9. American Psychological Association, "A Grateful Heart Is a Healthier Heart," April 9, 2015, http://www.apa.org/news/press /releases/2015/04/grateful-heart.aspx.

10. Alvin Powell, "Decoding Keys to a Healthy Life," *Harvard Gazette*, February 2, 2012, http://news.harvard.edu/gazette/story/2012/02 /decoding-keys-to-a-healthy-life/.

11. TED, "Robert Waldinger: What Makes a Good Life? Lessons from the Longest Study on Happiness," November 2015, http://www.ted .com/talks/robert_waldinger_what_makes_a_good_life_lessons _from_ the_longest_study_on_happiness.

12. Pursuit of Happiness, "How Do You Measure Happiness? The Top Questionnaires," http://www.pursuit-of-happiness.org/science -of-happiness/measuring-happiness/.

13. "The Science Behind the Smile," *Harvard Business Review*, January/ February 2012, https://hbr.org/2012/01/the-science-behind-the -smile.

14. Ibid.

15. Panova and Lleras, "Avoidance or Boredom."

16. Ding Li, "What's the Science Behind a Smile?," *Voices*, April 2, 2014, https://www.britishcouncil.org/voices-magazine/famelab -whats-science-behind-smile.

17. Leo Widrich, "The Science of Smiling: A Guide to the World's Most Powerful Gesture," Buffer, April 1, 2016, https://blog.buffer app.com/the-science-of-smiling-a-guide-to-humans-most -powerful-gesture.

18. Go Cognitive, "The Discovery of Mirror Neurons," http://www .gocognitive.net/interviews/discovery-mirror-neurons-1.

19. Ibid.

20. TED, "Ron Gutman: The Hidden Power of Smiling," March 2011, https://www.ted.com/talks/ron_gutman_the_hidden_power_of _smiling?language=en.

21. Deepak Chopra, Smita Malhotra, and Murali Doraiswamy, "Yoga and the Brain: A Vision of Possibilities," *Huffington Post*, June 21, 2015, http://www.huffingtonpost.com/deepak-chopra/yoga-and -the-brain-a-visi_b_7605504.html.

22. T. Gard, J. Noggle, C. Park, D. R. Vago, and A. Wilson, "Potential Self-Regulatory Mechanisms of Yoga for Psychological Health," *Frontiers in Human Neuroscience* 8 (2014), doi: 10.3389/ fnhum.2014.00770.

23. C. C. Streeter, P. L. Gerbarg, R. B. Saper, D. A. Ciraulo, and R. P. Brown, "Effects of Yoga on the Autonomic Nervous System, Gamma-Aminobutyric-Acid, and Allostasis in Epilepsy, Depression, and Post-Traumatic Stress Disorder," *Medical Hypotheses* 78 (2012): 571–579.

24. Timothy McCall, "38 Health Benefits of Yoga" Yoga Journal, August 28, 2007, http://www.yogajournal.com/article/health/count -yoga-38-ways-yoga-keeps-fit.

25. Heart of Yoga, "Mobile Apps," http://www.heartofyoga.com/apps.

26. Dana Santas, "Be Happier with 7 Minutes of Yoga," CNN, June 12, 2015, http://www.cnn.com/2015/06/12/health/yoga-happiness.

27. YJ Editors, "5 Happiness Boosting Poses," Yoga Journal, August 13, 2013, http://www.yogajournal.com/beginners/5-happiness -boosting-poses.

28. Davidji, "Leading a Purpose Driven Life with Meditation," Heal Your Life, April 4, 2016, http://www.healyourlife.com/leading-a -purpose-driven-life-with-meditation.

29. Sue McGreevey, "Eight Weeks to a Better Brain," *Harvard Gazette*, January 21, 2011, http://news.harvard.edu/gazette/story/2011/01 /eight-weeks-to-a-better-brain.

30. Eco Institute, "Why Meditation Makes You So Happy," http://eocinstitute.org/meditation/meditation-and-happiness-why-meditation-makes-you-so-happy.

31. "TEDxBoulder — Shannon Paige — Mindfulness and Healing," YouTube video, 16:52, posted by "TEDx Talks," October 18, 2012, https://www.youtube.com/watch?v=UcGUo6uNs34.

32. Kira M. Newman, Tom Jacobs, Mariah Flynn, Summer Allen, Jill Suttie, Jason Marsh, Jeremy Adam Smith, and Emiliana R. Simon-Thomas, "The Top 10 Insights from the 'Science of a Meaningful Life' in 2016," Greater Good, December 26, 2016, http://greatergood.berkeley.edu/article/item/the_top_10_insights_from_the_science_of_a_meaningful_life_in_2016.

33. Ibid.

34. Seligman, *Flourish*.

35. Peter Malinowski, "Meditation and Neuroplasticity: Five Key Articles," Meditation Research, March 4, 2014, http://meditation-research.org.uk/2014/03/meditation-and-neuroplasticity-five-key-articles/.

36. Christopher Bergland, "The Neurochemicals of Happiness," *Psychology Today*, November 29, 2012, https://www.psychologytoday.com/blog/the-athletes-way/201211/the-neurochemicals-happiness.

Chapter 4: Living with Purpose, Living with Love

1. Blankets for the Homeless, http://www.blanketsforthehomeless.org.

2. A. L. Burrow and P. L. Hill, "Purpose as a Form of Identity Capital for Positive Youth Development," *Developmental Psychology* 47 (2011): 1196–1206.

3. E. S. Kima, V. J. Strecherb, and C. D. Ryff, "Purpose in Life and Use of Preventive Health Care Services," *Proceedings of the National Academy of Sciences of the United States of America* 111 (2014): 16331–16336.

4. R. G. Tedeshi and L. G. Calhoun, *Posttraumatic Growth: Conceptual Foundation and Empirical Evidence* (Philadelphia: Lawrence Erlbaum Associates, 2004).

5. TED, "Jane McGonigal: The Game That Can Give You 10 Extra Years of Life," June 2012, http://www.ted.com/talks/jane_mcgonigal_the_game_that_can_give_you_10_extra_years_of_life.

6. Papá Jaime, http://www.papajaime.com/en.

7. El Sistema USA, http://www.elsistemausa.org.

8. TED, "Jose Abreu: The El Sistema Music Revolution," February 2009, http://www.ted.com/talks/jose_abreu_on_kids_transformed_by_music?language=en#t-916347.

9. "Incredible high school musicians from Venezuela! | Gustavo Dudamel," YouTube video, 17:06, posted by "Ted," February 19, 2009, http://www.youtube.com/watch?v=amSqQ5XNaGE.

10. Unite for Sight, http://www.uniteforsight.org.

11. "Jennifer Staple-Clark: 'Quality Impact: What It Takes to Grown a Successful Organization,'" YouTube video, 21:09, posted by "uniteforsight," March 3, 2014, http://www.youtube.com/watch?v=vRn9L8n4H00.

12. Pencils of Promise, http://www.pencilsofpromise.org.

13. Adam Braun, http://www.adambraun.com.

14. Adam Braun, *Promise of a Pencil* (New York: Scribner, 2015).

15. Grameen Bank, http://www.grameen-info.org.

16. S. Achor, *The Happiness Advantage: The Seven Principles of Positive Psychology That Fuel Success and Performance at Work* (New York: Crown Business, 2010), 175.

Chapter 5: Gratitude as an Anchor

1. Helen Russell, "How to Start a Gratitude Practice to Change Your Life," Tiny Buddha, http://tinybuddha.com/blog/how-to-start-a-gratitude-practice-to-change-your-life.

2. Jason Marsh, "Tips for Keeping a Gratitude Journal," Greater

Good, November 17, 2011, http://greatergood.berkeley.edu/article/item/tips_for_keeping_a_gratitude_journal.

3. Positive Psychology News, "Gratitude and Forgiveness," http://positivepsychologynews.com/image-maps/positive-emotions/gratitude-and-forgiveness.

4. Advanced Life Skills, "Gratitude Is Among the Top Advanced Life Skills," http://advancedlifeskills.com/blog/allow-gratitude-to-transform-your-life.

5. Arthur C. Brooks, "Choose to Be Grateful. It Will Make You Happier," *New York Times*, November 21, 2015, http://www.nytimes.com/2015/11/22/opinion/sunday/choose-to-be-grateful-it-will-make-you-happier.html.

6. Robert Emmons, "The New Science of Gratitude," Gratitude Power, http://gratitudepower.net/science.htm.

7. Amy Morin, "7 Scientifically Proven Benefits of Gratitude That Will Motivate You to Give Thanks Year-Round," *Forbes*, November 23, 2014, http://www.forbes.com/sites/amymorin/2014/11/23/7-scientifically-proven-benefits-of-gratitude-that-will-motivate-you-to-give-thanks-year-round/#398fe5f56800.

8. Oliver Sacks, *Gratitude* (New York: Knopf, 2015).

9. Martin, "The Google Way of Motivating Employees," Cleverism, September 25, 2014, https://www.cleverism.com/google-way-motivating-employees/.

10. Susan Heitler, "Does Gratitude Matter in Marriage?," *Psychology Today*, July 14, 2012, https://www.psychologytoday.com/blog/resolution-not-conflict/201207/does-gratitude-matter-in-marriage.

11. Patty Onderko, "5 Ways to Raise a Grateful Child," *Parenting*, http://www.parenting.com/article/5-ways-to-raise-a-grateful-child.

12. Jason Marsh and Dacher Keltner, "Thanksgiving and Gratitude: The Science of Happier Holidays," *Wall Street Journal*, November 28, 2014, http://www.wsj.com/articles/thanksgiving-and-gratitude-the-science-of-happier-holidays-1417183949.

13. Sean Robertson, "A Culture of Gratitude," *Beijing Review*, February 13, 2014, http://www.bjreview.com.cn/eye/txt/2014-02/10/content_594944.htm.

14. Kim Weiss, "7 Ways to Express Gratitude Around the World," mindbodygreen, November 21, 2014, http://www.mindbodygreen.com/0-16218/7-ways-to-express-gratitude-around-the-world.html.

15. Paula Vasan, "How Parents Express Love in Different Parts of the World," *Huffington Post*, April 5, 2015, http://www.huffingtonpost.com/paula-vasan/how-parents-express-love-in-different-parts-of-the- world_b_6511164.html.

16. Carolyn Gregoire, "Buddhist Teacher Jack Kornfield on Gratitude, the Mindful Revolution, and Learning to Embrace Suffering," *Huffington Post*, May 5, 2015, http://www.huffingtonpost.com/2014/05/05/buddhist-teacher-jack-kor_n_5249627.html.

17. Mayo Clinic, "Resilience: Build Skills to Endure Hardship," http://www.mayoclinic.org/tests-procedures/resilience-training/in-depth/resilience/art-20046311.

18. Eric Barker, "10 Ways to Boost Your Emotional Resilience, Backed by Research," *Time*, April 26, 2016, http://time.com/4306492/boost-emotional-resilience/.

19. Wayne Dyer, "Resilient," Wayne Dyer's website, http://www.drwaynedyer.com/blog/tag/resilient/.

20. Maria Konnikova, "How People Learn to Become Resilient," *New Yorker*, February 11, 2016, http://www.newyorker.com/science/maria-konnikova/the-secret-formula-for-resilience.

21. Lao Tzu, *Tao Te Ching*, trans. Stephen Mitchell (New York: Harper & Row, 1988).

22. "Survivor of Auschwitz Death Camp Reveals Her 'Bittersweet Memories,'" YouTube video, 10:44, posted by "Heart Beings," March 10, 2016, https://www.youtube.com/watch?v=cnAlH_URMog.

23. Shannon M. Greene, Edward R. Anderson, E. Mavis Hetherington,

Marion S. Forgatch, and David S. DeGarmo, "Risk and Resilience after Divorce," in *Normal Family Processes: Growing Diversity and Complexity*, 3rd edition, ed. Froma Walsh (New York: Guilford Press, 2003), http://psycnet.apa.org/psycinfo/2003-04409-004.

24. Jane E. Brody, "Getting on with Life after a Partner Dies," *New York Times*, June 14, 2010, http://www.nytimes.com/2010/06/15/health/15brod.html.

25. Abraham P. Greeff, Alfons Vansteenwegen, Tina Herbiest, "Indicators of Family Resilience after the Death of a Child," *OMEGA—Journal of Death and Dying* 63, no. 4 (December 2011): 343–358, https://www.researchgate.net/publication/51729319_Indicators_of_Family_Resilience_ after_the_Death_of_a_Child.

26. Clare Ansberry, "Resilience Can Be Learned," *Wall Street Journal*, March 24, 2015, http://www.wsj.com/articles/after-loss-how-to-learn-resilience-1427225009.

27. Pursuit of Happiness, "Viktor Frankl," http://www.pursuit-of-happiness.org/history-of-happiness/viktor-frankl/.

28. Emily Esfahani Smith, "A Psychiatrist Who Survived the Holocaust Explains Why Meaningfulness Matters More Than Happiness," *Huffington Post*, October 23, 2014, http://www.huffingtonpost.com/2014/10/23/meaningfulness-happiness-viktor-frankl_n_6034052.html.

29. Brian Cain, "10 Life Lessons from *Unbroken*," Brian Cain's website, http://briancain.com/blog/10-life-lessons-from-unbroken.html.

Chapter 6: Daily Practices for a More Purposeful You

1. Marjorie Fiske Lowenthal, "Social Isolation and Mental Illness in Old Age," *American Sociological Review* 29, no. 1 (February 1964): 54–70, http://www.jstor.org/stable/2094641?seq=1#page_scan_tab_contents.

2. Carla M. Perissinotto, Irena Stijacic Cenzer, and Kenneth E. Covin-

sky, "Loneliness in Older Persons: A Predictor of Functional Decline and Death," Archives of Internal Medicine 172, no. 14 (2012):
1078–1084, http://jamanetwork.com/journals/jamainternalmedi
cine/fullarticle/1188033.

3. Rebecca G. Adams, "Friendship—How Friends Influence the
Lives of Older Adults," Medicine Encyclopedia, http://medicine
.jrank.org/pages/660/Friendship-How-friends-influence-lives
-older-adults.html.

4. Stephen G. Post, "Altruism, Happiness, and Health: It's Good to
Be Good," International Journal of Behavioral Medicine 12, no. 2
(June 2005): 66–77, http://link.springer.com/article/10.1207/s153
27558ijbm1202_4.

5. Meredith Melnick, "The Age-Defying Benefits of Having Older
(and Younger) Friends," Huffington Post, May 6, 2014, http://www
.huffingtonpost.com/2014/05/06/heres-why-you-should-seek_n
_5120705.html.

6. http://www.thepowerofforgiveness.com/understanding/index
.html

7. Ibid.

8. Dr. Wayne W. Dyer, "How to Forgive Someone Who Has Hurt
You: In 15 Steps," http://www.drwaynedyer.com/blog/how-to
-forgive-someone-in-15-steps/

9. Lori Deschene, "How to Forgive Someone When It's Hard: 30
Tips to Let Go of Anger," http://tinybuddha.com/blog/how-to
-forgive-someone-when-its-hard-30-tips-to-let-go-of-anger/.

10. http://www.thepowerofforgiveness.com/understanding/index
.html

11. Yuna L. Ferguson and Kennon M. Sheldon, "Trying to Be Happier
Really Can Work: Two Experimental Studies," Journal of Positive
Psychology 8, no. 1 (2013): 23–33, http://www.tandfonline.com/doi
/abs/10.1080/17439760.2012.747000#.VRG7iZPF-nS.

12. Michael D. Lemonick, "Why Your Brain Craves Music," Time,
April 15, 2013, http://science.time.com/2013/04/15/music/.

13. "Want to Boost Your Mood? Try listening to Prince, Bob Marley and the Beach Boys," *Daily Mail*, January 23, 2013, http://www .dailymail.co.uk/sciencetech/article-2267125/Want-boost-mood -Try-Listening-Prince-Beach-Boys.html.

14. Lauren Davidson, "This is the Kind of Music You Should Listen to at Work," *Telegraph*, June 2, 2016, http://www.telegraph.co.uk /business/2016/06/02/this-is-the-kind-of-music-you-should -listen-to-at-work/.

15. Anne J. Blood and Robert J. Zatorre, "Intensely Pleasurable Responses to Music Correlate with Activity in Brain Regions Implicated in Reward and Emotion," *Proceedings of the National Academy of Sciences of the United States of America* 98, no. 20 (2001): 11818–11823, http://www.pnas.org/content/98/20/11818.SHORT.

16. K. I. Erickson and A. F. Kramer, "Aerobic Exercise Effects on Cognitive and Neural Plasticity in Older Adults," *British Journal of Sports Medicine* 43 (2009): 22–24, http://bjsm.bmj.com/content /43/1/22.short.

17. Christopher Bergland, "Why Is Physical Activity So Good for Your Brain?," *Psychology Today*, September 22, 2014, https://www .psychologytoday.com/blog/the-athletes-way/201409/why-is -physical-activity-so-good-your-brain.

18. Ibid.

19. Stephanie Castillo, "The Happiness Trick You Haven't Tried," *Prevention*, November 21, 2012, http://www.prevention.com/mind -body/emotional-health/dancing-shown-help-boost-happiness -and-mental-health

20. Lane Anderson, "Mind Your Body: Dance Yourself Happy," *Psychology Today*, June 9, 2016, https://www.psychologytoday.com /articles/201007/mind-your-body-dance-yourself-happy.

21. Dana Santas, "Be Happier with 7 Minutes of Yoga," CNN, June 12, 2015, http://www.cnn.com/2015/06/12/health/yoga-happiness.

22. Theresa E. DiDonato, "5 Reasons Why Couples Who Sweat Together, Stay Together," *Psychology Today*, January 10, 2014, https://

www.psychologytoday.com/blog/meet-catch-and-keep/201401/5 -reasons-why-couples-who-sweat-together-stay-together.

23. M. Stel, and R. Vonk, "Mimicry in Social Interaction: Benefits for Mimickers, Mimickees, and their Interaction," *British Journal of Psychology* 101, no. 2 (2010): 311–323.

24. Giovanni, "Types of Meditation—An Overview of 23 Meditation Techniques," Live and Dare, January 28, 2015, http://liveanddare .com/types-of-meditation/.

25. "Buddhist Meditation," *Wikipedia*, last updated May 22, 2017, https://en.wikipedia.org/wiki/Buddhist_meditation.

26. Giovanni, "Types of Meditation."

27. Holistic Living, "Meditation Techniques—Taoist Meditation Methods," http://1stholistic.com/meditation/hol_meditation_taoist _meditation.htm.

28. Giovanni, "Contemplative Prayer and Christian Meditation," Live and Dare, http://liveanddare.com/contemplative-prayer-and -christian-meditation/.

29. UCLA Mindful Awareness Research Center, "Free Guided Meditations," http://marc.ucla.edu/mindful-meditations.

Chapter 7: Seven Simple Steps to a Happier You

1. Invisible Gorilla, "Gorilla Experiment," http://theinvisiblegorilla .com/gorilla_experiment.html

2. Dalai Lama Quotes, "We Are but Visitors . . . ," http://www.dalaila maquotes.org/we-are-but-visitors-on-this-planet-we-are-here -for-ninty-or-one-hundred-years-at-the-very-most-during-that -period-we-must-try-to-do-something-good-something-useful -with-our-lives-if-you/.

Epilogue

1. Edmund Hillary.

INDEX